BLACK&DECKER®

THE COMPLETE GUIDE TO

CUSTOM SHELVES &
BUILT-INS

Build Custom Add-ons to
Create a One-of-a-Kind Home

by Theresa Coleman

Creative Publishing
international

CHANHASSEN, MINNESOTA
www.creativepub.com

Creative Publishing
international

Copyright © 2007
Creative Publishing international, Inc.
18705 Lake Drive East
Chanhassen, Minnesota 55317
1-800-328-3895
www.creativepub.com
All rights reserved

Printed at R.R. Donnelley

10 9 8 7 6 5 4 3 2

Library of Congress Cataloging-in-Publication Data

Coleman, Theresa.
  The complete guide to custom shelves & built-ins : build custom add-ons to create a one-of-a-kind home / by Theresa Coleman.
    p. cm.
  At head of title: Black & Decker.
  Summary: "More than 30 step-by-step projects to help homeowners achieve custom built-ins that add function and style to any home decor"--Provided by publisher.
  Includes index.
  ISBN-13: 978-1-58923-303-4 (soft cover)
  ISBN-10: 1-58923-303-4 (soft cover)
  1. Built-in furniture. 2. Cabinetwork. 3. Shelving (Furniture) I. Title. II. Title: Black & Decker the complete guide to shelves & built-ins.

  TT197.5.B8C59 2007
  684.1'6--dc22

2007010500

President/CEO: Ken Fund
VP for Sales & Marketing: Peter Ackroyd

Home Improvement Group

Publisher: Bryan Trandem
Managing Editor: Tracy Stanley
Senior Editor: Mark Johanson
Editor: Jennifer Gehlhar

Creative Director: Michele Lanci-Altomare
Senior Design Manager: Brad Springer
Design Managers: Jon Simpson, Mary Rohl

Director of Photography: Tim Himsel
Lead Photographer: Steve Galvin
Photo Coordinators: Julie Caruso, Joanne Wawra
Shop Managers: Randy Austin, Bryan McClain

Production Managers: Laura Hokkanen, Linda Halls

Page Layout Artist: Danielle Smith
Photographer: Joel Schnell
Shop Help: Dan Anderson, Glenn Austin, Tami Helmer, John Webb

The Complete Guide to Custom Shelves and Built-Ins
Created by: The Editors of Creative Publishing international, Inc., in cooperation with Black & Decker.
Black & Decker® is a trademark of The Black & Decker Corporation and is used under license.

NOTICE TO READERS

For safety, use caution, care and good judgment when following the procedures described in this book. The Publisher and Black & Decker cannot assume responsibility for any damage to property or injury to persons as a result of misuse of the information provided.

The techniques shown in this book are general techniques for various applications. In some instances, additional techniques not shown in this book may be required. Always follow manufacturers' instructions included with products, since deviating from the directions may void warranties. The projects in this book vary widely as to skill levels required: some may not be appropriate for all do-it-yourselfers, and some may require professional help.

Consult your local Building Department for information on building permits, codes and other laws as they apply to your project.

Contents

The Complete Guide to Custom Shelves & Built-Ins

Introduction

Get ready to flex your carpentry muscles and improve your home with a little help from stock and semi-stock cabinets.

Built-ins are no longer just for kitchens. With the range of available cabinet sizes, finishes, and organization accessories available in stock and semi-stock styles, combining cabinets and standard sheet goods to create custom looks for your favorite rooms is a realistic option to buying the pre-made shelves and hutches that everyone else in your neighborhood owns.

We designed the one-of-a-kind projects in this Complete Guide to live up to the essence of the title—"complete"—without making the projects too tough for weekend DIYers. The result: A variety of fun projects for various skill levels with a range of design styles for rooms all over your house.

If you like the look of sleek urban style, check out The Club Bar (page 168). Its slick modular palette is a total attention grabber that you might find in an avant-garde city hotel. The classically appointed Formal Bookcase (page 188), on the other hand, is DIY-friendly project inspired by traditional hardwood libraries.

Chasing the brass ring of good design inspired more than just a hip-traditional design stew. It begged us to be mindful of the permanence of these projects. Sure, the projects are fun to create, but we took the nature of a built-in seriously. When you create a built-in or add shelving, it becomes part of your home, part of your day-to-day reality—whether your built-in is used to store laundry detergent, display cherished mementos, or curl up with a favorite book.

We crafted projects that you can build, projects with rock-solid, real-world assembly and fabrication techniques. And, since many of the designs include semi-stock cabinets, the carpentry skills needed aren't

Built-ins are more than just simple shelves and wall cabinets. Whether you are building a cozy kitchen nook (left), an underbed platform (below) or a storage cabinet that custom-fits your bathroom floorplan (right), unique little extras like drawers and cubbies in one-of-a-kind built-in furniture can maximize storage options for every type of space.

Bookshelves are one of the most popular types of built-in projects. Bookshelves don't have to just be showcased prominently in a formal living room, they also fit perfectly—and dramatically maximize smaller homes' storage potential—along hallways (opposite page). Built-in storage also can act as a visual room divider in larger spaces, creating the opportunity to display keepsakes that can be viewed from both rooms, and giving homeowners additional nooks to stow other items away (left). Even the smallest, simplest of shelves can greatly increase the amount of usable space (below) and add visual impact.

Built-in projects aren't just for traditionalists. In the built-ins category you will find countless perfect projects and stock products that match the modern style of many of today's homes. A uniquely shaped room can benefit from a custom built-in couch that maximizes the space inside the frame. Drawers keep throw blankets handy for colder days, and games ready for guests. A kitchen with a view is a perfect spot to integrate an eating area without interrupting the floorplan or flow of the space. And for the home office, there are many cabinets that offer semi-stock accessories, from file drawers and CD organizers to pull-out writing trays and office supply organization trays (right).

The bathroom (opposite page) is a smaller space in most homes, and really benefits from some custom built-in organization. Optimizing the space with a built-in cabinet outfitted with upgraded organization accessories can help keep all of those little bottles and grooming supplies much more easily managed.

Sports equipment, shoes, and coats are typically among the top clutter culprits in most houses. By creating a coat cubby or locker-room-styled organization (below) near the most-used entryway, you'll create a greater chance that those items might be put away. For kids' rooms, take advantage of the whimsy of color and style when decorating custom built-ins, and take the opportunity to maximize the storage possibilities (left).

Awkward spaces, nooks and crannies don't offer much utility to the homeowner, but when improved with a clever built-in or shelving project, the space can become a real asset for your home. Understairs areas are prime examples of unused space that can be exploited with a built-in, as with this understairs wine rack (right).

If your idea of built-ins is simply cabinet installations in a kitchen or a bathroom, there are many styles, finishes, and colors available. Cabinet-makers are offering detailing options—moldings, wine racks, spice racks, and pull-out trays, for example—that help you create the exact look and performance you desire (below).

TECHNIQUES
& DESIGN

Tools & Materials

Building shelves and built-ins is a challenging job that requires patience, attention to detail, and the right tool for each task. Without these basic requirements, you are setting yourself up for potential failure and the result will suffer.

Start off right by using high-quality tools. Good tools last longer and are generally more accurate than less expensive versions.

Many people buy tools only as they are needed to avoid purchases they will not use. This rationale should only apply to power tools and higher-priced specialty items. A high-quality basic tool set is important for every do-it-yourselfer to have on hand. Doing so avoids improper tool usage and makes your job easier, with improved results.

The hand tools you will need for most finish carpentry jobs can be broken down into two types: layout tools and construction tools. It is common for most people to own construction tools, but to lack necessary layout tools for basic carpentry jobs.

Purchase the highest-quality layout tools you can afford. They are crucial for helping you avoid costly measuring and marking mistakes.

LAYOUT TOOLS

Layout tools help you measure, mark, and set-up perfect cuts with accuracy. Many layout tools are inexpensive and simply provide a means of measuring for level, square, and plumb lines. However, recent technologies have incorporated lasers into levels, stud finders, and tape measures, making them more accurate than ever before but, at a slightly higher price. Although these new tools are handy in specific applications, their higher price is not always warranted for the do-it-yourselfer.

- **A tape measure** is one of the most common tools around. The odds are good that you already own at least one. (If you are making frequent trips for building supplies, invest in a second tape that stays in your car.) Carpentry projects require a sturdy tape measure with a length greater than your longest stock. A 25-ft. tape measure has a wider and thicker reading surface than a 16-ft. variety, but either is adequate for most carpentry jobs. If you can't tell the difference between the smaller lines on a standard tape, consider purchasing an "Easy Read" variety. It is important to read the tape accurately.

"Easy Read" tape measure

Combination square

Levels

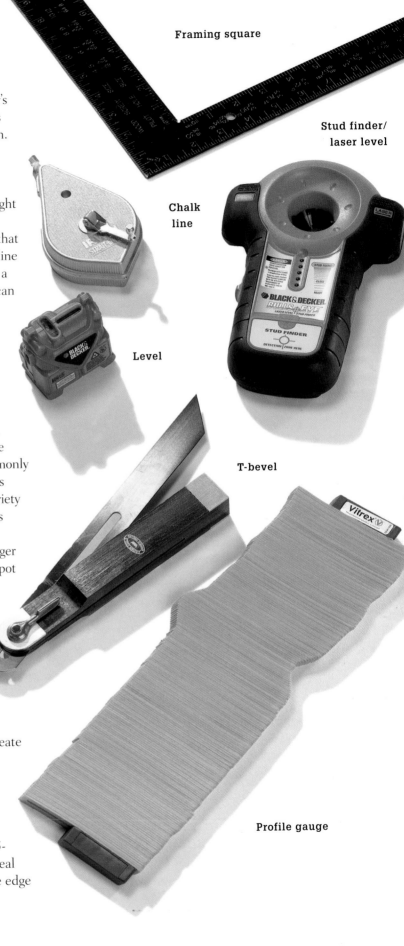

Framing square

Stud finder/laser level

Chalk line

Level

T-bevel

Profile gauge

- **A framing square,** also known as a carpenter's square, is commonly used to mark sheet goods and check recently installed pieces for position. Framing squares are also used as an initial check for wall squareness and plumb in relation to a floor or ceiling.

- **Chalk lines** are used to make temporary straight lines anywhere one is needed. The case of a chalk line, or the "box," is teardrop shaped so that the tool doubles as a plumb bob. Use a chalk line to mark sheet goods for cutting or to establish a level line in a room. Keep in mind that chalk can be difficult to remove from porous surfaces.

- **A stud finder** is used to locate the framing members in a wall or ceiling. Higher-priced versions also locate plumbing, electrical, or other mechanicals in the wall. Although stud finders are not completely necessary, they are convenient for larger jobs.

- **Levels** are available in a variety of lengths and price ranges. The longer and more accurate the level, the higher the price. The two most commonly used sizes are 2-ft. and 4-ft. lengths. 2-ft. levels are handy for tighter spaces, while the 4-ft. variety serves as a better all-purpose level. Laser levels are handy for creating a level line around the perimeter of a room or for level lines along longer lengths. They provide a wide range of line or spot placement, depending on the model.

- **A T-bevel** is a specialized tool for finding and transferring precise angles. T-bevels are generally used in conjunction with a power miter saw to gauge angled miters of non-square corners. This tool is especially handy in older homes where the original states of square, plumb, and level may no longer apply.

- **A profile gauge** uses a series of pins to recreate the profile of any object so that you may transfer it to a work piece. Profile gauges are especially useful when dealing with irregular obstructions.

- **A combination square** is a multifunction square that provides an easy reference for 45- and 90-degree angles, as well as marking reveal lines or a constant specific distance from the edge of a work piece.

CONSTRUCTION TOOLS

- **A good quality hammer** is a must for every carpentry project. A 16-oz. curved claw hammer, otherwise known as a finish hammer, is a good all-purpose choice. Some people prefer a larger straight claw hammer for heavy tear-down projects and rough framing, but these hammers are too clumsy and heavy for driving smaller casing and finish nails, and tend to mar the surface of trim.

- **Utility knives** are available in fixed, retracting, and retractable blades. This tool is used for a wide variety of cutting tasks from pencil sharpening to back-beveling miter joints. Always have additional blades readily available. Folding fixed-blade utility knives offer the durability and strength of a fixed blade with the protection of a folding handle.

- **A set of chisels** is necessary for installing door hardware as well as notching trim around obstacles and final fitting of difficult pieces. Keep a set only for use with wood, and do not substitute them for screwdrivers.

- **Block planes** are used to fit doors into openings and remove fine amounts of material from trim. A finely tuned block plane can even be used to clean up a sloppy miter joint.

- **A coping saw** has a thin, flexible blade designed to cut curves and is essential for making professional trim joints on inside corners. Coping saw blades should be fine toothed, between 16 and 24 teeth per inch for most hardwoods, and set to cut on the pull stroke of the saw to offer you more blade control.

- **A sharp handsaw** is convenient for quick cut-offs and in some instances where power saws are difficult to control. Purchase a crosscut saw for general-purpose cutting.

- **Protective wear,** including safety glasses and ear protection, is required any time you are working with tools. Dust masks are necessary when sanding, doing demolition, or when working around fumes.

- **Pry bars** come in a variety of sizes and shapes. A quality forged high-carbon steel flat bar is the most common choice. Wrecking bars make lighter work of trim and door removal due to their added weight. No matter what type of pry bar you use, protect finished surfaces from scratches with a block of wood when removing trim.

- **Side cutters and end nippers** are useful for cutting off and pulling out bent nails. The added handle length and curved head of an end nippers makes them ideal for larger casing nails.

Pneumatic brad nails and smaller pins will pull out easier with side cutters. Purchase a nail set for countersinking nail heads. Three-piece sets are available for different nail sizes.

- **A rasp and metal file set** is important for fitting coped joints precisely. The variety of shapes, sizes, and mills allow for faster rough removal of material, or smoother slow removal, depending on the file.

- **Use a putty knife** to fill nail holes with wood filler and for light scraping tasks.

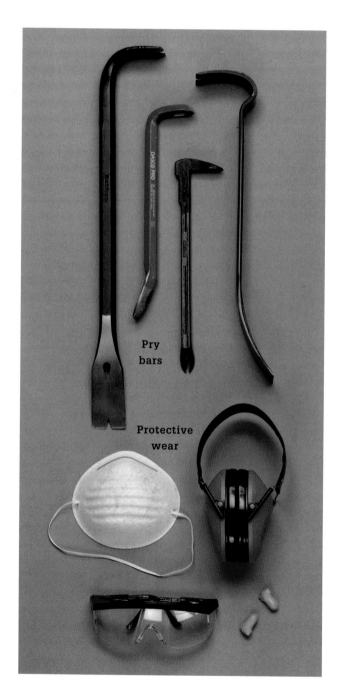

Pry bars

Protective wear

Putty knife

Handsaws

Nail sets

Hammer

Utility knives

Coping saw

Rasp and metal file set

Side cutters and end nippers

Block plane

Chisels

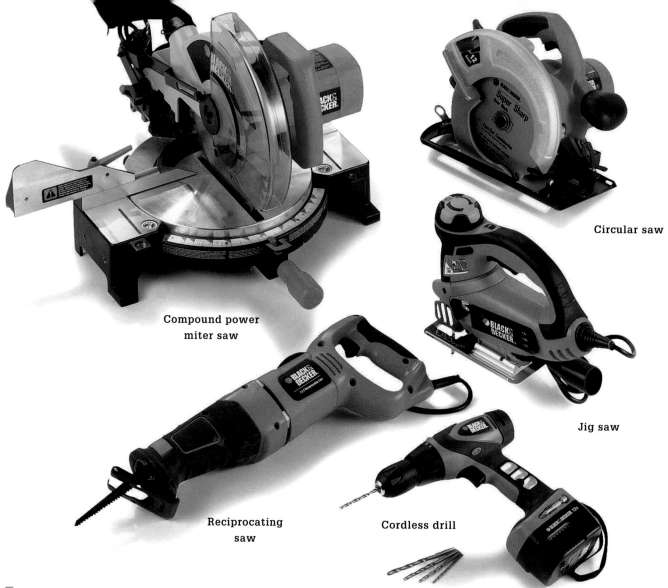

Compound power
miter saw

Circular saw

Jig saw

Reciprocating
saw

Cordless drill

Power Tools

Despite the higher price as compared to hand tools, power tools are a great value. They allow you to work more quickly and accurately than with hand tools and make repetitive tasks like sanding, drilling, and sawing more enjoyable. Basic home carpentry does not require every power tool shown here, but some tools, such as a power miter box, are crucial for professional results. Purchase power tools on an as-needed basis, keeping in mind that while the cheapest tool is not always your best option, the most expensive and powerful is probably not necessary, either. Cheaper tools generally sacrifice precision, while the most expensive tools are made for people who use them every day, not just occasionally.

- **A cordless drill** is one of the handiest tools available. Although drills are not normally used to install trim, they make quick work of installing structural components. Occasionally, trim-head screws are used to install trim, rather than nails or regular wood screws.
- **A circular saw** is ideal for straight cuts in plywood and quick cut-offs of solid material. Purchase a plywood blade to make smooth cuts in plywood, and a general-purpose blade for other cuts.
- **A jig saw** is the perfect tool for cutting curves, or notching out trim around obstructions. Jig saw blades come in an array of designs for different styles of cuts and different types and thicknesses of materials. Always use the right type of blade and do not force the saw during the cut or it may bend or break.

Router

Random orbit sander

Biscuit joiner

Power planer

Finish sander

Belt sander

Table saw

- **A biscuit joiner** (also called a plate joiner) is a specialty tool used for alignment and to make strong joints between two square pieces of stock.
- **A reciprocating saw** is used for removal and tear-down applications. This tool is especially handy for removing door jambs.
- **A power miter saw, or chop saw,** will yield professional results. Most have a 10" or 12" diameter blade. A compound power miter saw has a head that pivots to cut both bevels and miters. Sliding miter saws have more cutting capacity but are less portable. A fine-tooth carbide-tipped blade is best for built-in and shelving projects.
- **A belt sander** is not essential but is a handy tool for quick removal of material.
- **Random-orbit sanders** are a good choice for smoothing flat areas, such as plywood, quickly.

Random-orbit sanders leave no circular markings, like a disc sander, and can sand in any direction regardless of wood grain.

- **Finish sanders** are available in a variety of sizes and shapes for different light sanding applications.
- **A power planer** is used to trim doors to fit openings and flatten or straighten out materials. Power planers are faster to use than manual hand planes, but the results are more difficult to control.
- **A table saw** is the best tool for ripping stock to width, and larger models can be fitted with a molding head for cutting profiles.
- **A router** (plunge router is shown here) has many uses in trim carpentry, especially for cutting edge profiles to make your own custom workpieces.

Pneumatic Tools

Pneumatic tools can be a key to timely, professional carpentry results. They save time and energy over traditional hammer-and-nail installation. Not only do they drive fasteners quickly, but they countersink at the same time, avoiding multiple strikes to trim, which could throw joints out of alignment. Predrilled holes are not necessary with pneumatic tools. Splitting is infrequent if the work piece is held firmly in place

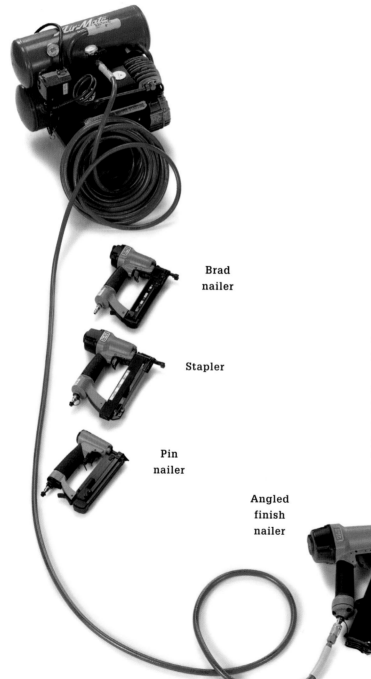

Brad nailer

Stapler

Pin nailer

Angled finish nailer

and the nails are positioned at least 1" from trim ends. Nail guns also allow you to concentrate on the placement of the work piece with one hand and fasten it with the other. You needn't fumble around with single fasteners because they are already loaded in the gun.

The costs of pneumatic tools, compressors, and fasteners has decreased over the years, making them not only the professional's choice, but a great option for the do-it-yourselfer as well. Pneumatic kits are available at home centers with two different guns and a compressor at a value price. For small or infrequent jobs, consider renting pneumatics.

Portable compressors are available in different styles, including pancake and hot-dog styles. Any compressor with air pressure capability of 90 psi or greater will drive a finish or brad nailer. Consider options like tank size, weight of the unit, and noise levels while the compressor is running. Talk to a home center specialist about what your specific compressor needs are and keep in mind any future pneumatic tools you might want.

The two basic pneumatic tools used in carpentry are a finish nailer, and a brad nailer. A finish nailer drives 15-gauge nails ranging from 1" to 2½". These nails work for a variety of moldings, door and window trim, and general-purpose fastening. Angled finish nailers are easier to maneuver in tight corners than straight guns, but either option will work. Brad nailers drive smaller 18-gauge fasteners ranging in length from ½" to 2". Some brad nailers' maximum length is 1¼". Because the fasteners are smaller, it is no surprise that the gun is lighter and smaller than a finish gun. Brad nailers are used to attach thinner stock, with less tendency to split the wood. Headless pinners drive fasteners similar to brad nails, but without the head. These nails have less holding power, but are normally used to hold small moldings in place until the glue dries. Be sure to load headless pins with the points down, taking note of the label on the magazine. ⅜" crown staplers are used to attach thin panels and in situations where maximum holding power is needed, but the fastener head will not be visible. Because staples have two legs and a crown that connects them, their holding power is excellent. However, the hole left by the staple's crown is large and can be difficult to conceal.

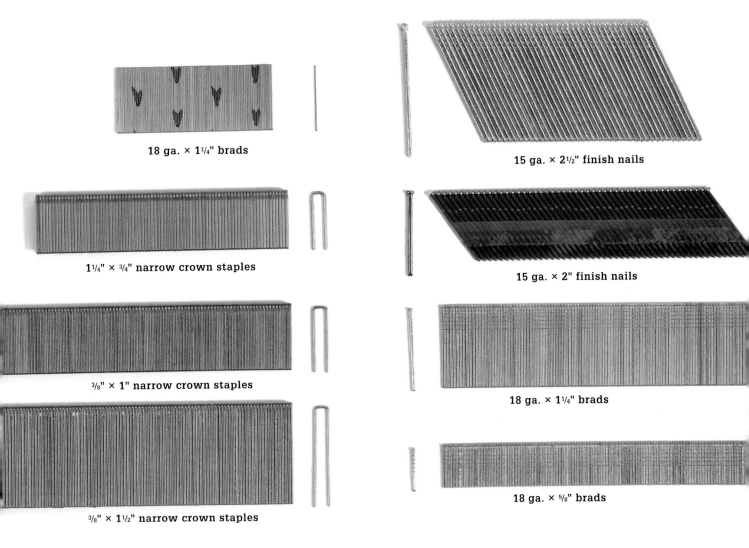

18 ga. × 1¼" brads

15 ga. × 2½" finish nails

1¼" × ¾" narrow crown staples

15 ga. × 2" finish nails

⅜" × 1" narrow crown staples

18 ga. × 1¼" brads

⅜" × 1½" narrow crown staples

18 ga. × ⅝" brads

Pneumatic Fasteners

15-gauge angled finish nails and regular finish nails range in length up to 2½". The angled variety are exactly the same as the straight nails, but come in angled clips. These nails are made from galvanized wire, so they are suitable for exterior applications. Use finish nails to attach larger moldings and trim casings. Drive fasteners at regular intervals along the moldings and keep the position of the nails at least 1" from the molding ends. Fastener length is dependent upon the size of workpiece installed. Typical stock moldings and dimensional lumber is ¾" thick. When installing built-ins, the fastener must pass through the molding and wallboard and into the stud behind. Generally, half the fastener should be embedded in the backing or stud, so in most applications, 2" fasteners should suffice.

18-gauge brad nails range in length up to 2" for some guns and leave smaller holes to fill than finish guns. Brad nails are commonly used for thinner casings that are nailed directly to a solid backer. A specific example of this is along the inner edge of a door or window casing. The outer edge of the trim is nailed with a finish gun through the wallboard, while the inside edge rests against the door jamb, so it can be fastened with a brad nailer. Headless pins leave almost no nail hole to fill but are limited in length to 1". Their holding power is greatly diminished due to the lack of head, but they are generally used in conjunction with wood glue. ⅜" crown staples are used only when the fastener head will not be visible.

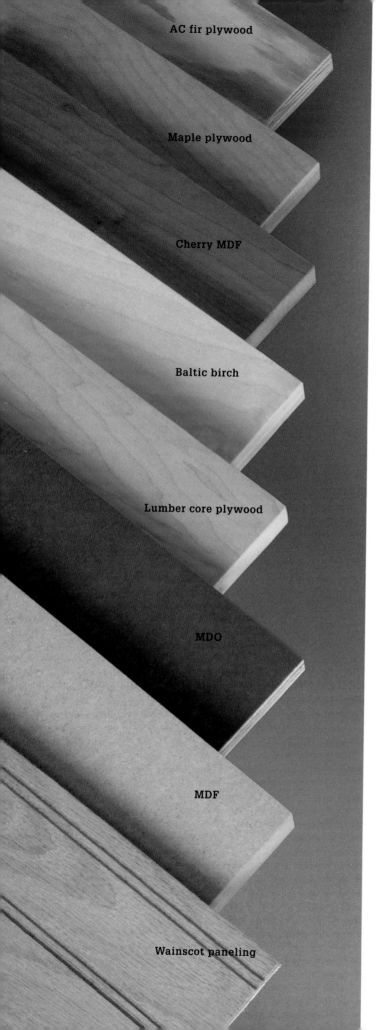

AC fir plywood

Maple plywood

Cherry MDF

Baltic birch

Lumber core plywood

MDO

MDF

Wainscot paneling

Sheet Goods

There are many different types of plywood for a wide array of uses. For built-in and shelf projects, finish-grade or paint-grade plywood is commonly used. Each type is made up of thinly sliced layers called plies. These layers are made of solid hardwood, softwood, or wood products. The more plies a sheet good has, the stronger it will be. This is only true for veneer-based plies. Medium density fiberboard, or MDF, is made of wood fibers that have been glued and pressed together. These panels are extremely stable and rarely shrink, expand, or warp. Plywood thicknesses range from 1/8" to 1". Many species of wood are available for the outer plywood veneers. Therefore, the core, or inner plies, give the panel its structural characteristics.

3/4" or 23/32" AC plywood has a finish-grade face on one side and a utility grade on the other. Standard AC plywood is made of seven plies of softwood, such as spruce or pine. This plywood is a good choice for paint-grade moldings. 3/4" hardwood veneer plywood is available in red oak, maple, and birch at most home centers. Its inner core is basically the same as AC plywood, but it has a hardwood outer face. 3/4" MDF oak veneer plywood is made up of three layers: two outer oak veneers and a solid core made of MDF. This plywood tends to be less expensive than a veneer core product and has a smoother face, but is heavy, less durable, and does not hold fasteners as well.

MDF is available with or without an outer veneer. 3/4" Baltic birch plywood is made up of thirteen plies, making it more dimensionally stable than regular veneer core plywood. This panel is commonly used in Modern-style trim and can be painted or stained. Lumber-core plywood has strips of solid wood edge-glued between outer veneer plies. Medium density overlay, or MDO, plywood has a solid wood veneer core with an MDF face. This panel eliminates the weight of a MDF panel and has the fastening strength of a solid veneer core. The MDF face is perfect for paint-grade applications. Wainscoting paneling is available in several thicknesses from 3/16" to 5/8".

Lumber

Solid hardwood is available at most home centers in varying widths. Species vary, depending on your location. These boards make good solid stock material to combine with or mill into new trim moldings because they are already planed to a uniform thickness. If you can't find the type of lumber you need at a home center, check with a lumberyard or a small cabinet shop in your area. For larger runs with a uniform thickness, many cabinet shops will charge a nominal flat fee to plane the boards for you. They may even be willing to order the material for you through a local distributor.

Tip ▶

Whenever possible, do a quick inspection of each board before you purchase it. Because hardwood lumber is often stained, carefully take note of cosmetic flaws such as splits, knots, checks, and wanes. These issues can sometimes be cut around, but once the finish is applied, the imperfection will show through. Lumber that is twisted, cupped, or crooked should not be used at full length. If a board is slightly bowed, you can probably flatten it out as you nail it. In any case, always choose the straightest, flattest lumber you can find.

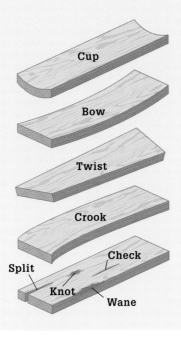

Planning a Project

With any of the built-in and shelf projects found in this book, you can either build the project as shown, or adapt the design to fit your unique space and needs. To build the project as shown, follow the measurements in the parts table that accompanies each project. Small width and height adjustments can be made using the fitting tips on page 32.

When adapting a built-in design, it is very important to make accurate plan drawings on graph paper to show how the project will fit in your space. These drawings let you organize your work and find approximate measurements for parts; they also make it easier to estimate the cost of materials.

To ensure a professional look and functional use, plan your built-ins so they fall within the standard range of sizes used by cabinet makers and furniture manufacturers (page opposite.)

Whether you are adapting a project or following a design as shown, it is safer to measure and cut the pieces as you assemble the built-in in its location, rather than to precut all pieces in advance. Small discrepancies in marking, cutting, and assembly techniques can lead to costly errors if you precut all the pieces.

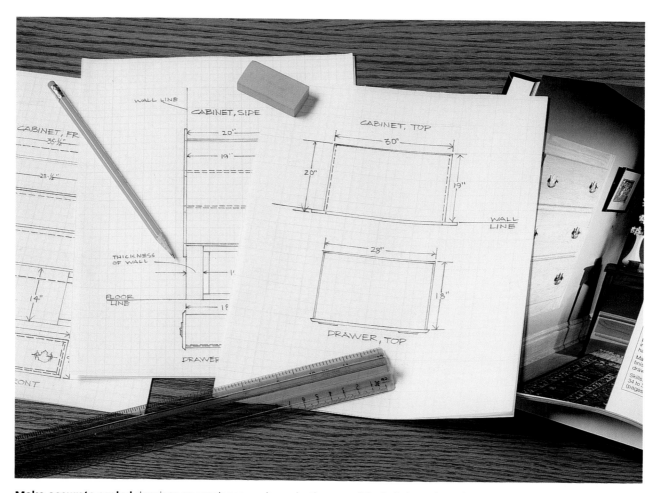

Make accurate scaled drawings on graph paper when adapting one of the built-in projects featured in this book. Use a simple scale, like 1 square = 1", to draw a side, top, and one or more front views of your project. For a complicated project, draw several front views showing the basic walls (carcase) of the built-in, the face frame construction, and the finished project including drawers and doors. Side views and top views should show all trim pieces and moldings. Make sure to use the actual measurements of sheet goods and dimension lumber when making your drawings.

STANDARD BUILT-IN MEASUREMENTS

Highest shelf should be no more than 80" above the floor to be within easy reach.

Shelves should be at least 10" deep in bookcases, and 12" deep in hanging wall cabinets. Space the shelves so there is at least ½" of open space above the items you are storing.

First shelf in a wall-hung built-in should be at least 18" above a countertop.

Work-surface height varies depending on how the surface is used. Place the surface 28" to 30" above the floor for a typing desk or sewing work center. Place the countertop at 36" for standard kitchen cabinets, at 44" for a dry bar or eating counter, or at 34" for accessible rooms.

Standard seating surfaces, like window seats and desk chairs, are between 16" and 20" high.

Base cabinet depth varies from 15" for a room divider to 30" for cabinets that support a desk surface. Standard kitchen-style floor cabinets usually are 24" or 25" in depth.

Access space in front of a built-in should be at least 36" to provide kneeling space for opening drawers and cabinet doors.

Drawer sizes range from a minimum of 3" high, 8" wide, and 8" deep; to a maximum of 10" high, 36" wide, and 30" deep. Large drawers, more than 24" wide, should be equipped with two drawer slides for stability.

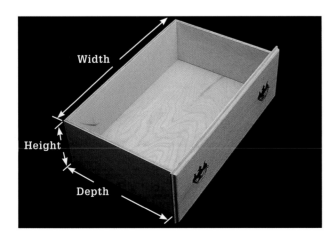

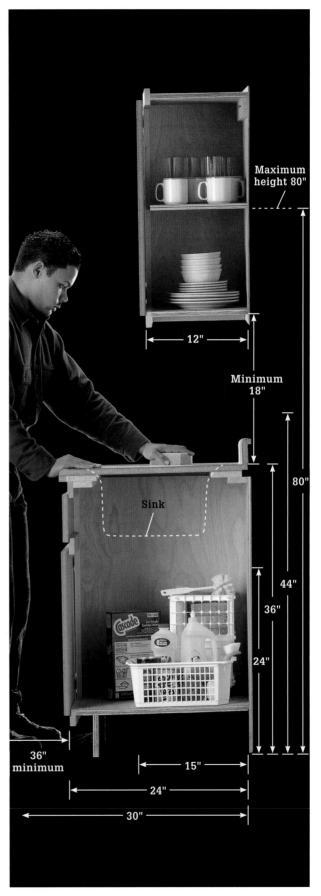

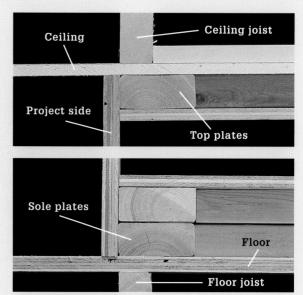

Ceiling

Ceiling joist

Project side

Top plates

Sole plates

Floor

Floor joist

Filler strip

Face frame

Make small width adjustments (up to 6" on each side) with hardwood strips measured and cut to fill the extra space. Attach the strips to the edges of the face frame with counterbored wood screws. These "filler strips" let you slightly enlarge a project without making changes to the basic design. Filler strips also can be scribed to fit uneven walls.

Make small height adjustments by changing the thickness of the sole plates or top plates that anchor the built-in to the floor and ceiling. The floor-to-ceiling projects in this book are designed to fit rooms with 8-ft. ceilings. If your room height differs slightly, adjusting the sole plates or top plates lets you adapt a project without major design changes.

Nominal size	Actual size
1 × 2	¾" × 1½"
1 × 3	¾" × 2½"
1 × 4	¾" × 3½"
1 × 6	¾" × 5½"
1 × 8	¾" × 7¼"
2 × 4	1½" × 3½"
2 × 6	1½" × 5½"
2 × 8	1½" × 7¼"
2 × 10	1½" × 9¼"

Measure spaces carefully. Floors, walls, and ceilings are not always level or plumb, so measure at several points. If measurements vary from point-to-point, use the shortest measurement to determine the height or width of your built-in.

Measure your materials. Actual thickness for plywood can vary from the listed nominal size; ¾" plywood, for example, can vary in thickness by nearly ⅛".

Use actual measurements, not nominal measurements, of dimension lumber when planning a built-in. The table above shows the actual dimensions of common lumber.

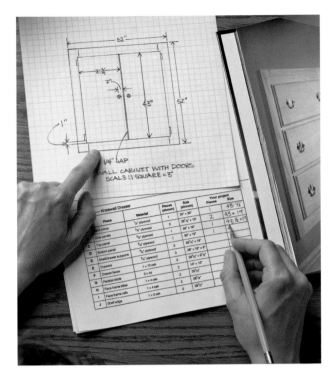

Revise the listed measurements of a featured project, if necessary, and record them. Use your scaled drawings as a guide for estimating the revised measurements. Always double-check measurements before cutting pieces to prevent costly cutting errors.

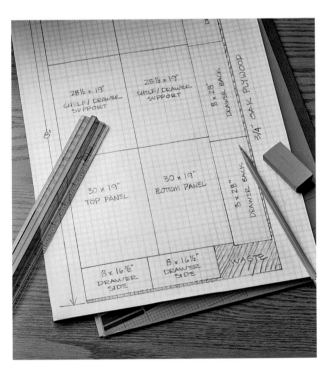

Make cutting diagrams to help you make efficient use of materials. Make scale drawings of sheet goods on graph paper, and sketch cutting lines for each part of your project. When laying out cutting lines, remember that the cutting path (kerf) of a saw blade usually consumes ⅛" of wood.

Materials	Amount needed	Cost for each	Total cost
Plywood (4 ft. x 8 ft.)			
¼" sheets			
½" sheets			
¾" sheets			
Lumber			
1 × 2 boards			
1 × 3 boards			
1 × 4 boards			
1 × 6 boards			
1 × 8 boards			
2 × 4s			
Moldings			
Door-edge			
Shelf-edge			
Base shoe			
Baseboard			
Crown/cove			
Ornamental			
Hardware			
Finish nails			
Power-drive screws			
Angle brackets			
Countertop brackets			
Drawer slides			
Hinges			
Door latches			
Pulls/knobs			
Other materials			
Wood glue			
Oil/stain			
Sanding sealer			
Paint			
Outlet strips			
Grommets			
Light fixtures			

Total cost:

Make a list of materials, using your plan drawings and cutting diagrams as a guide. Photocopy this materials list, and use it to organize your work and estimate costs.

Jobsite Preparation

Whether you are installing an elaborate, custom built-in or a simple shelf, preparing the jobsite is an important step of your project. Remove furniture and other objects from the rooms you will be working in so that you won't worry about getting sawdust on a nice upholstered chair, or accidentally damaging an antique furnishing. Cover any items you cannot remove with plastic sheeting. You may also want to cover finished floors with cardboard or plastic as well, to protect them from scratches or just to make clean-up easier.

Set up tools such as a power miter saw at a central workstation, to avoid walking long distances between where you are installing and where you are cutting material. This central location is key to professional results because measurements are easier to remember and quick trimming is possible without the added time of exiting and entering the house.

Make sure the work area is well lit. If you don't already own one, purchase a portable light (trouble light) to make viewing the workpieces easier. Keep your tools sharp and clean. Accidents are more likely when blades are dull and tools are covered in dust and dirt.

Keep the work area clean and organized. A dedicated tool table for staging your tools is a great organizational aid. Tool tables also make it possible to conveniently keep tools from disappearing. If you only use the tools that you need and set them on the tool table when you aren't using them, tools stay off the floor and out of other rooms. Add a set of clamps to the table and you have a convenient space for fine-tuning the fit of each piece.

Organize your tools and avoid wearing a bulky work belt by setting up a dedicated tool table where all of your project tools and materials can be staged.

In some built-in or shelving projects, the most efficient way to accomplish the work is to convert the installation room into a temporary workshop.

Project Safety

Personal safety should be a priority when working on any project. Power tools and hand tools can cause serious injuries that require immediate attention. Be prepared for such situations with a properly stocked first aid kit. Equip your kit with a variety of bandage sizes and other necessary items such as antiseptic wipes, cotton swabs, tweezers, sterile gauze, and a first aid handbook.

To help you avoid using the first aid kit, read the owner's manuals of all power tools before operating them, and follow all outlined precautions. Protect yourself with safety glasses, ear protection, and dust masks and respirators when necessary.

Keep your work environment clean and free of clutter. Clean your tools and put them away after each work session, sweep up dust and any leftover fasteners, and collect scraps of cut-off trim in a work bucket. These scraps may come in handy before the end of the project, so keep them around until you are finished.

Maintain safety throughout your project, and remember that being safe is a priority. Everyone needs to use ear protection when operating loud tools. If you don't, you will lose your hearing. People don't just get used to loud noise. They lose their hearing and the noise doesn't seem as loud. The concept that safety applies to everyone but you is foolish. Take the necessary precautions to prevent injury to yourself and those around you.

Always wear safety glasses and ear protection when operating power tools. Use dust masks when necessary, and protect yourself from chemicals with a respirator. Work gloves save your hands when moving or handling large amounts of material. Knee pads are useful when working on floor-level projects such as baseboard.

Read the owner's manual before operating any power tool. Your tools may differ in many ways from those described in this book, so it's best to familiarize yourself with the features and capabilities of the tools you own. Always wear eye and ear protection when operating a power tool. Wear a dust mask when the project will produce dust.

Cutting & Fitting Joints

Cutting and fitting joints is a skill that requires patience, knowledge, and well-maintained equipment to achieve effective results. There are a few basic joints that are generally used for most carpentry applications: butt, inside and outside miter, scarf, and coped joints.

Although cutting joints accurately is the key function of a power miter saw, it is not the only tool necessary for quality joinery. Coped joints require a coping saw as well as a set of metal files. For some applications, fitting butt joints is simplified with the use of a biscuit jointer or a pocket hole jig. These are specialty tools designed for joining wood.

Cutting and fitting joints during installation can be very frustrating, especially when it involves difficult walls that are not plumb and corners that are out of square. Take the time to read through the proper techniques of using a miter saw, as well as the correct method for cutting each individual joint. These techniques are described in detail to help you work through the imperfections found in every house and to avoid common problems during installation.

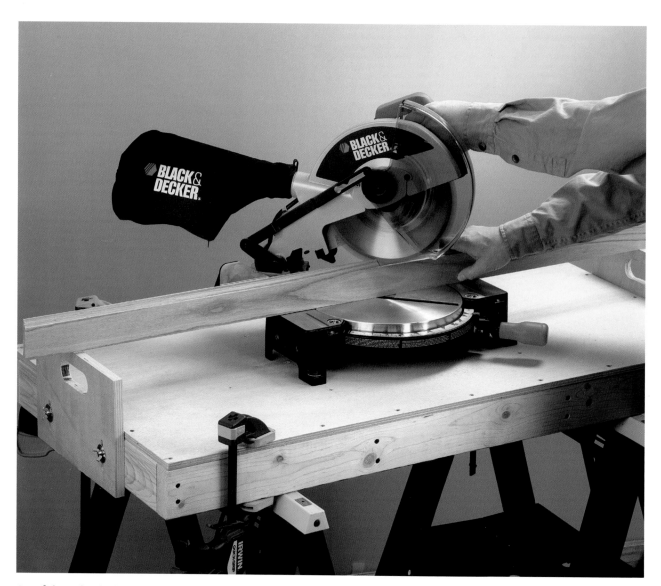

Careful cutting is the hallmark of good joinery, be it in making furniture or installing trim moldings. Used correctly, a power miter saw offers the speed and precision to make your project look like it was done by a pro.

Power Miter Saw Techniques

There are two main types of power miter saws. The basic style cuts mitered angles when material is placed against the fence or beveled angles when material is placed flat on the work surface. The second type is called a compound miter saw. Compound saws allow you to cut a miter and a bevel simultaneously. The compound angle is extremely helpful in situations where a corner is out of plumb and a mitered angle requires a bevel to compensate. Some compound saws are available with a sliding feature that allows you to cut through wider stock with a smaller blade size. This option raises the cost of the saw considerably.

Tip: To avoid cutting off too much, start out by making a cut about ¼" to the waste side of the cutting line, then nibble at the workpiece with one or more additional cuts until you have cut up to the cutting line. Wait until the blade stops before raising the arm on every cut.

Tips for Cutting with a Power Miter Saw ▸

To cut multiple pieces of stock to the same length, clamp a stop block to your support table at the desired distance from the blade. After cutting the first piece, position each additional length against the stop block and the fence to cut pieces of equal length.

Make a full downward cut with a compound saw to cut wide stock. Release the trigger and let the blade come to a full stop, then raise the saw arm. Flip the workpiece over and finish the cut.

Use a sliding miter saw equipped with a saw carriage that slides away from the fence. These saws have greater cutting capacity than a nonsliding saw so they can cut wider stock. They're also more expensive, but you may find it worth renting one.

Mitering Outside Corners

Cutting outside miters is one of the main functions of a power miter saw. Most saws have positive stops (called detents) at 45° in each direction, so standard outside corners are practically cut for you by the saw. Keep in mind that your saw must be accurately set up to cut joints squarely. Read the owner's manual for setting up your saw as well as for safety precautions. Before you begin, check the walls for square with a combination square or a framing square. If the corner is very close to square, proceed with the square corner installation. If the corner is badly out of square, follow the "Out of Square" procedure on the following page.

Tools & Materials ▸

Combination square
  or framing square
Miter saw
Pencil
Tape measure
Pneumatic finish nail gun

Air compressor
Air hose
T-bevel
Molding
Masking tape
1 × 4

How To Miter Square Outside Corners

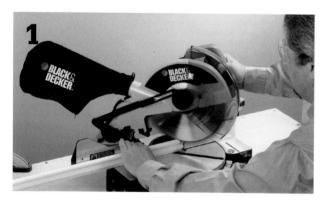

1

Set the miter saw to 45°. Position the first piece on-edge, flat on the miter box table, flush against the fence. Hold the piece firmly in place with your left hand and cut the trim with a slow, steady motion. Release the power button of the saw and remove the molding after the blade stops.

2

Set the miter saw blade to the opposing 45° positive stop. Place the second piece of molding on-edge, flat on the saw table, flush against the fence. Fasten the piece tightly in place with a hold-down or clamp. Cut the molding with a slow, steady motion.

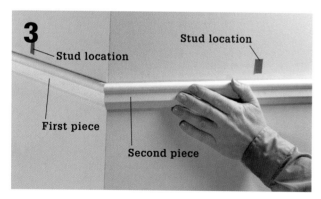

3

Stud location

Stud location

First piece

Second piece

With the first piece of molding tacked in place, hold the second piece in position and check the fit of the joint. If the joint is tight, nail both pieces at stud locations.

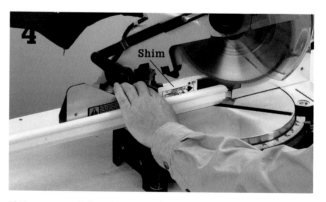

4

Shim

If the corner joint does not fit tightly, shim the work piece away from the fence to make minor adjustments until the joint fits tightly. Shims should be a uniform thickness. Playing cards work well.

How to Miter Out-of-Square Outside Corners

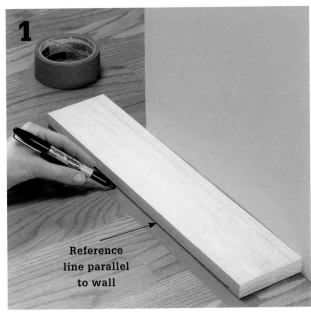

Draw a reference line off each wall of the corner using a straight 1 × 4. Put masking tape down on the finished floor to avoid scuffing it and to see your lines clearly. Trace along each wall, connecting the traced lines at a point out from the tip of the corner.

To find the angle you need to miter your moldings, place a T-bevel with the handle flush against one wall, and adjust the blade so that it intersects the point where your reference lines meet. Lock the blade in place at this angle.

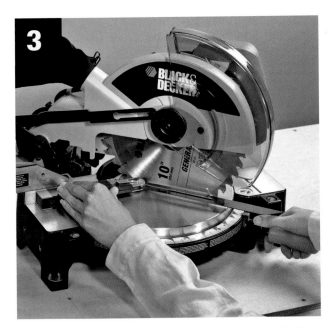

Transfer the angle of the T-bevel to the miter saw by locking the saw in the down position and adjusting the angle to match the angle of the T-bevel.

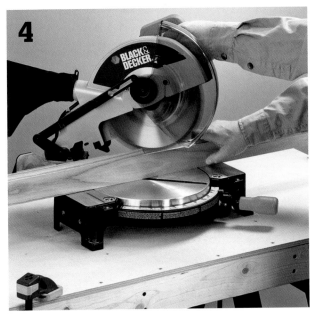

Position the molding on-edge, flat on the saw table and flush against the fence. Cut at your cutting mark. Tack the workpiece in place and repeat steps 2 through 4 to measure and cut the mating piece. Or, you can subtract the angle of the first cut (for example, 47°) from 90° to find the angle for the second cut (43° in this case). Using math is faster; taking direct measurements is more reliable.

Mitering Inside Corners

Although most professionals prefer to cope-cut inside corners, it is common to see moldings that are mitered to inside corners. These joints are more likely to separate over time and to allow gaps to show. For that reason it is not advised to use inside corner miters when installing a stain-grade trim product. The gaps will be visible and are very difficult to fill with putty. For paint-grade projects, mitering inside corners makes more sense because joints can be filled and sanded before the top coats of paint are applied.

Tools & Materials ▸

Miter saw	Pneumatic finish nail gun
Pencil	Air compressor
Tape measure	Air hose
Utility knife	Molding

How To Miter Square Inside Corners

Set the miter saw to 45° and place the first piece of trim on-edge, flat on the miter box table and flush against the fence. Hold the piece firmly in place with your left hand and cut the trim with a slow, steady motion. Release the power button and remove the molding after the blade stops.

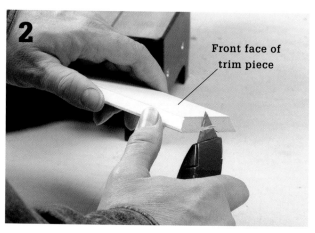

Front face of trim piece

Back-cut the inside edge of the trim piece with a utility knife so that the top corner will sit flush against the wall corner.

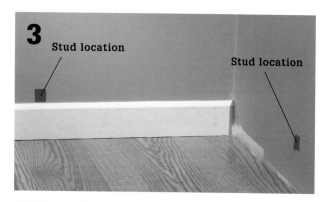

Stud location

Stud location

Butt the molding tightly against the wallboard and tack it into place.

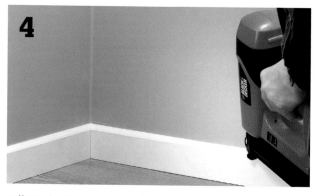

Adjust the blade of the miter saw to the opposite 45° angle and cut the mating piece. Test the fit of the joint, adjusting the miter angle if necessary. Once the fit is tight, nail both pieces at stud locations.

Building a Straightedge Guide

Making straight and accurate cuts on plywood or paneling is a challenge. Even the best carpenter can't always keep the blade on the cut line, especially over a longer span. A straightedge guide solves this problem as long as you keep the saw's base plate flush with the edge of the cleat.

The cleated edge of the guide provides an accurate anchor for the base plate of the saw as the blade passes through the material. You can make a straight cleat edge by ripping the first 2" off of an existing plywood panel and using the factory edge. Use a fine-toothed blade for rip cuts and a plywood blade for splinter-free crosscuts.

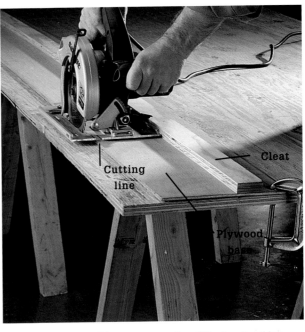

A **straightedge guide** overcomes the difficulty of making square rip cuts and other square cuts on long workpieces. The guide is built square, ensuring that any cuts made with it will be square as well.

Tools & Materials ▸

C-clamps
Pencil
Circular saw
¼" Plywood base (10 × 96")

¾" Plywood
cleat (2 × 96")
Carpenter's
glue

How to Build a Straightedge Guide

1

Apply carpenter's glue to the bottom of the ¾" plywood cleat, then position the cleat on the ¼" plywood base, 2" from one edge. Clamp the pieces together until the glue dries.

2

Position the circular saw with its foot tight against the ¾" plywood cleat. Cut away the excess portion of the plywood base with a single pass of the saw to create a square edge.

3

To use the guide, position it on top of the workpiece, so the guide's square edge is flush with the cutting line on the workpiece. Clamp the guide in place with C-clamps.

Cutting Mitered Returns

Mitered returns are a decorative treatment used to hide the end grain of wood and provide a finished appearance. Mitered returns range from tiny pieces of base shoe up to very large crown moldings. They are also commonly used when installing a stool and apron treatment or on decorative friezes above doors.

Bevel returns are another simple return option for chair rail, baseboard, and base shoe. A bevel return is simply a cut at the end of the molding that "returns" the workpiece back to the wall at an angle. The biggest advantage to using mitered returns rather than bevel returns is that mitered returns already have a finished surface. Bevel returns require more touchups.

Cutting mitered returns for small moldings, such as quarter-round, or for thin stock, such as baseboard, can be tricky when using a power miter saw. The final cut of the process leaves the return loose where it can sometimes be thrown from the saw due to the air current of the blade. Plan on using a piece of trim that is long enough to cut comfortably, or you will find yourself fighting the saw.

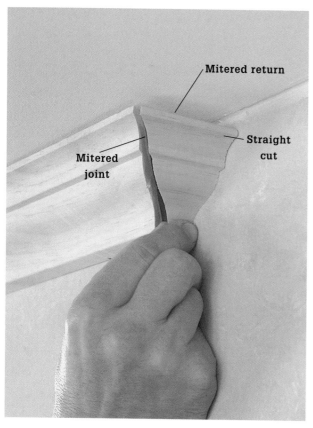

Mitered returns finish molding ends that would otherwise be exposed. Miter the main piece as you would at an outside corner. Cut a miter on the return piece, then cut it to length with a straight cut so it butts to the wall. Attach the return piece with wood glue.

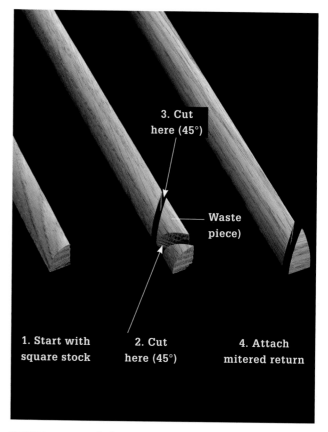

Returns are made from two 45° angle cuts. The scrap piece is removed and the return piece is glued into place.

How to Cut Mitered Base Shoe Returns

Measure and mark the molding to length. Adjust the miter saw blade to 45° and back-miter the molding, cutting the front edge to the desired overall length of the trim. Nail the back-mitered piece in place using a square to line it up flush with the edge of the door casing.

Adjust the blade of the miter saw to the opposite 45° angle and miter-cut the molding using a slow, steady stroke.

Mitered return

Mitered return

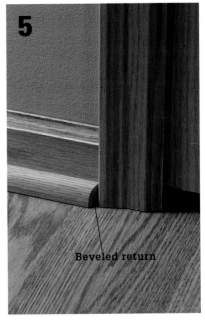

Beveled return

Hold the mitered molding against the baseboard at a right angle above the installed base shoe. Mark the molding at the depth of the installed base shoe. Square-cut the molding at the cutoff mark. Because making this cut with a power saw is very dangerous, use a miter box and a back saw. The cut-off piece will be the mitered return piece.

Check the fit of the return against the baseboard. If it is too small, repeat steps 3 and 4, making the piece slightly larger. If the return is too large, trim it to fit with a utility knife or sandpaper. Once the return fits properly, glue it in place with wood glue.

OPTION: Beveled returns are a quick and simple alternative to mitered returns. They require finish touchup after the trim is installed.

Establishing Level, Plumb & Square

Good carpenters strive to achieve three basic ideals in their work: plumb, level, and square. Go into any home, however, and you are bound to find walls that bow, floors that slope, and corners that don't form right angles. This doesn't always mean the carpenter did a poor job, but rather reflects the fact that wood and many building materials are natural products that expand, contract, and settle with the seasons. These natural movements do not always occur at the same rate, however, causing fluctuations that sometimes become permanent. That's why it's no surprise that older homes more commonly have larger fluctuations.

These movements can make trimming a built-in project challenging. Level and plumb are hard concepts to apply when the floor slopes heavily and corners float in or out. Compounding the problem further is that power tools are made to cut and shape wood precisely. Preset angles on a compound miter saw don't include angles such as 47 degrees.

In most cases, your installation of built-ins and trim will require compromises. Keep in mind the overall appearance of your project and remember that the concepts of plumb and level can be relative concepts. Strive to achieve them for quality joints, but don't insist on them when they affect the overall appearance of your project negatively. Here are a couple of fine pieces of advice to keep in mind:

- Level to the room is more important than level to the earth.
- Flat is more important than level.

A plumb bob is hung to establish a plumb (exactly vertical) line. Plumb can be difficult to visualize. Most chalk boxes can double as plumb bobs for rough use.

Window and door jambs are normally installed level and plumb, but if they aren't your casing should still follow an even reveal of 3/16" to 1/4" (about the thickness of a nickel) around the inside edge. Set the blade on a combination square to the depth of the reveal, then use the square as a guide for your pencil when marking. Install the casings flush with the mark.

Use a spacer block as a guide to install moldings near a ceiling. The spacer will allow you to easily follow any ups and downs of an uneven ceiling, making the trim run parallel to it rather than exactly level.

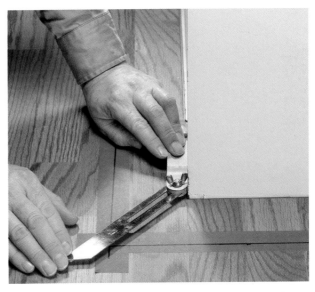

Install baseboard as close to level as possible, paying attention to areas where a floor dips or slopes over a longer length. In these instances, "cheat" the baseboard as close to level as you can, leaving a gap below it. You can only cheat the molding to less than the height of your base shoe, or quarter round. These trim pieces will cover the gap because they are thinner and easier to flex to the contour of your floor. Cheating the molding will also make cutting miters easier because they will require less of a bevel.

Use a T-bevel to measure for miter-cutting trim on out-of-square corners. Use a piece of scrap 1 × 4 to trace lines parallel to the corner walls. Place the T-bevel so the blade runs from the corner of the wall to the point where the lines intersect. Transfer this angle to your miter saw to cut your moldings.

Adding Doors

Cabinet doors are easy to make using ½" finish-grade plywood, and door-edge moldings. When hung with semi-concealed overlay hinges, do-it-yourself panel-style doors require no complicated routing or mortising techniques. You can build them to any size needed, and finish them to match your tastes.

Another easy option is to buy ready-made cabinet doors from a cabinet manufacturer or cabinet refacing company, and hang them yourself using semi-concealed hinges. You also can have a professional cabinetmaker design and build custom cabinet doors to your specifications—a good choice if you want wood-framed doors with glass panels.

Other do-it-yourself door options include sliding doors, solid-glass doors, and frameless doors (page opposite).

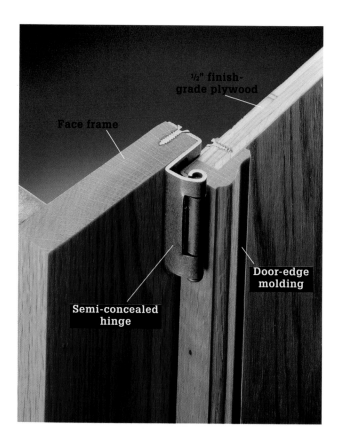

Easy-to-build overlay doors, made with ½" finish-grade plywood panels framed with door-edge moldings, are designed to overhang the face frame by about ⅜" on each side. Semi-concealed overlay hinges, which require no mortising, are attached to the back of the door and to the edge of the face frame. This door style also can be adapted to make folding doors.

Door-catch hardware is recommended if your doors do not use self-closing hinges, or if you want to lock them. Common types of hardware include: utility hasp (A), roller catch (B), keyed lock (C), brass door bolt (D), and magnetic push latch (E) commonly used for solid glass doors.

Door Options

Ready-made cabinet doors are available in stock sizes from cabinet manufacturers and cabinet refacing companies. Or, you can have doors custom-built by a professional cabinetmaker. Install these doors with semi-concealed overlay hinge.

Sliding doors are a good choice if limited space makes it impractical to install swinging doors. Build a pair of sliding doors from ¼" finish-grade plywood, cut so they are ½" shorter than the opening and will overlap by about 2" in the center. Attach door-track moldings to the top, bottom, and sides of the door opening. Install the doors by sliding them up into the top track, then lowering them into the bottom track.

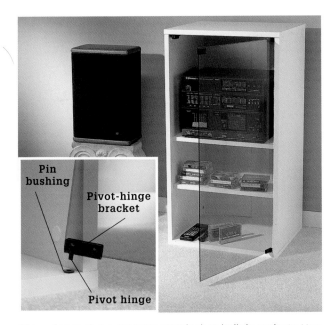

Pin bushing

Pivot-hinge bracket

Pivot hinge

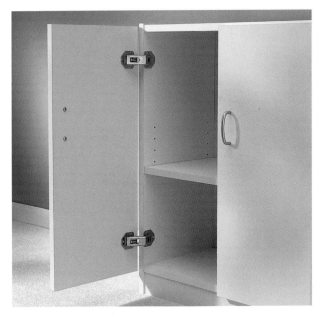

Glass doors give a contemporary look to built-in projects. Use ¼" tempered glass with smoothed edges, not ordinary window glass, for doors. To install a glass door, drill holes in the top and bottom of the door opening, and insert pivot-hinge bushings. Mount the door using pivot-hinge brackets attached to the glass with setscrews (inset).

Frameless doors are common on contemporary-style built-ins constructed without face frames — especially those made with melamine-covered particleboard. Frameless doors are mounted with concealed hinges attached to the inside surface of the built-in.

Basic Drawers

In its simplest form, a drawer is nothing more than a wooden box that slides in and out on a permanent shelf. Adding drawer slide hardware, a hardwood drawer face, and ornamental knobs or pulls makes drawers look more professional.

The drawer shown on the following page is simple to build and will work for any of the projects in this book. The design is called an "overlay" drawer because it features a hardwood drawer face that overhangs the cabinet face frame.

Ready-made hardwood drawer faces are sold by companies specializing in cabinet refacing products. You can also make your own drawer faces by cutting hardwood boards to the proper size and using a router with an edging bit to create a decorative flair.

A center-mounted drawer slide attached to the bottom of the drawer allows the drawer to glide smoothly and acts as a support for drawers installed in open cabinets.

The height, width, and depth of the cabinet, and the opening for the drawer must be carefully measured before the drawer is built, to ensure a good fit.

Directions: Overlay Drawer

INSTALL THE DRAWER TRACK
Install the track for the drawer slide, following the manufacturer's directions. If the slide will be supported by the face frame and the back panel, mount it using the rear bracket included with the slide kit. If the track will rest on a shelf, install it before the cabinet is assembled.

BUILD THE DRAWER FRAME
Measure the interior dimensions of the face frame and the depth of the cabinet from the back edge of the face frame to the interior surface of the back panel. Then follow the dimensions listed in the table (opposite page) to cut the drawer pieces to size.

Tip: Measuring the Cabinet ▶

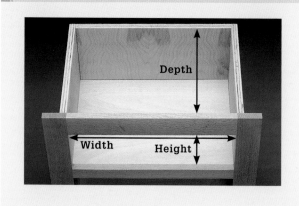

Part		Dimension
Sides	length	Depth of opening, minus 3"
	height	Height of opening, minus ½"
Front	length	Width of opening, minus 1½"
	height	Height of opening, minus ½"
Back	length	Width of opening, minus 1½"
	height	Height of opening, minus 1"
Bottom	length	Width of opening, minus 1"
	height	Depth of opening, minus 2¾"
Face	length	Width of opening, plus 1"
	height	Height of opening, plus 1"

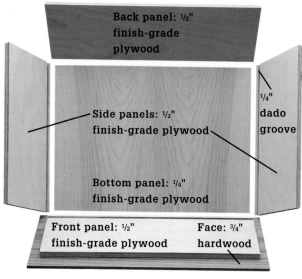

The basic overlay drawer is made using ½" plywood for the front, back, and side panels, and ¼" plywood for the bottom panel. The bottom panel fits into a ¼" dado near the bottom of the front and side panels, and is nailed to the bottom edge of the back panel. The hardwood drawer face is screwed to the drawer front from inside the drawer box.

1

Outline ¼"-wide dado grooves on the interior faces of the front and side panels. Rout ¼"-deep dado grooves along the marked outlines, using a router with a ¼" straight bit and a straightedge guide.

Clamp and glue the drawer panels together with the front and back panels between the side panels and the top edges of the panels aligned. Reinforce the joints with 2" finish nails driven through the front and back into the side panels.

ATTACH THE DRAWER BOTTOM

Let the glue dry and remove the clamps. Slide the bottom panel into the dado grooves from the back of the drawer box. Do not apply glue to the dado grooves or the bottom panel.

Attach the back edge of the bottom panel to the back panel, using brad nails spaced every 4".

APPLY THE FINISHING TOUCHES

Finish the drawer face to match your project, and allow the finish to dry. Position the drawer box against the back side of the drawer face, so the face overhangs by ½" on the sides and bottom, and 1" on the top. Attach the face with 1" screws driven from inside the drawer box.

Attach the drawer slide insert to the drawer bottom, following the manufacturer's directions. Attach any drawer pulls or knobs as desired, and slide the drawer into the cabinet, making sure the drawer slide and insert are aligned.

Mount the track for the drawer slide with the rear bracket when installing a drawer in an open cabinet.

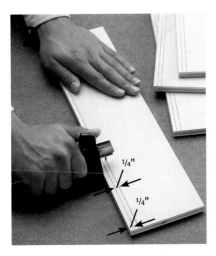

Outline and then rout a dado groove along the bottom edge of the front and side panels.

Slide the bottom panel into the dado grooves of the drawer assembly.

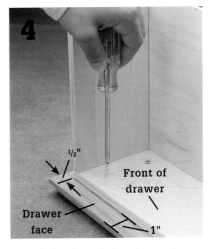

Attach the face of the drawer by driving screws through the front panel into the face.

Preparing for the Finish

A properly prepared wood surface absorbs finish materials evenly, focusing attention on the quality and color of the wood and the finish. A poorly prepared surface focuses attention on itself and its flaws.

Sanding or filling scratches and gouges, removing dents and stains, and carefully finish sanding are the essential steps in preparing for the finish. With many woods (especially softwoods like pine) you can create a more even finish by sealing the wood with sanding sealer immediately after finish sanding, then sanding the sealer lightly with 220-grit sandpaper after it dries. For exceptionally smooth, rich finishes (particularly on open-grain hardwoods like mahogany), apply wood grain filler to fill in checks and large pores, creating a smooth-as-glass surface.

Before beginning the final preparations for the finish, sand the workpiece with medium-grit sandpaper to remove small scratches and other surface problems—this is especially important if you did not use sanding as a final stage of finish removal. Any scratches, gouges, dents, or stains that survive the intermediate sanding should be remedied before you finish-sand.

Do your final stage of finish sanding immediately before you apply the finish—the smooth surface created by finish sanding is easily scratched or discolored.

Sand wood with power sanders, like the random-orbit sander shown above, to make quick work of the initial finish sanding stages, while producing a very smooth wood surface.

How to Prepare a Wood Surface

Get rid of glue. Dried glue won't absorb wood stain or any other penetrating coloring agents, so glue spills and squeeze-out show up as bright blotches if they're not removed by sanding or scraping before the finish is applied.

Sandpaper Grit Chart ▸

Grit	Task
80 to 100	Finish removal
120 to150	Preliminary finish sanding
180	Final sanding for softwood; intermediate stage of finish sanding for hardwood
220	Final sanding for hardwood
300 to 400	Sanding between finish layers
600 wet/dry	Wet sanding of final finish layer

Choose the right sandpaper for the job. Aluminum oxide and garnet are two common types. Aluminum oxide is a good general-use product suitable for most refinishing and finishing purposes. Garnet is usually cheaper than aluminum oxide, but it wears out much more quickly. Use sandpaper with the proper grit (higher numbers indicate finer grit—see chart above).

Apply wood grain filler that approximately matches the natural color of your wood. Available in light and dark colors, grain filler creates a smooth surface in open wood grains. Usually manufactured as a gel, it can be applied with a putty knife or a rag, but the excess material should be wiped off with a plastic scraper.

Make your own sanding sealer by blending one part clear topcoat material with one part topcoat solvent. *Note: Use the same topcoat material you plan to apply to the project. Sanding sealer is used before coloring soft or open-grain woods to achieve even stain penetration. To apply, wipe on a heavy coat, then wipe off the excess after a few minutes. Sand lightly with 220-grit sandpaper when dry.*

Surface Preparation

Surface preparation ensures an even, high-quality finish. Finish-sand with progressively finer grits of sandpaper, starting with 100-grit. Hardwood requires finer-grit sandpaper (a final sanding with 220-grit is common) than soft wood (sand to 150-grit). To speed up the process, use a power sander for the first stages of the sanding, then switch to hand-sanding to complete the process.

Finish sanding alone creates a smooth surface, but because wood absorbs stain at different rates, the color can be blotchy and dark. Sealing wood with sanding sealer (either a commercial product or your own concoction of thinned finish) evens out the stain-absorption rates and yields a lighter, more even finish. Filling the grain with a commercial paste filler creates a final finish that feels as smooth as it looks.

Use sanding sealer or grain filler for a fine finish. Finish sanding alone (left) can leave a blotchy surface when stain is applied, but a coat of sanding sealer (center) or grain-filler (right), or both, allows you to create a smoother, more even finish.

How to Finish-sand

Finish-sand all surfaces with 150-grit sandpaper, following the direction of the grain. Use a finishing sander on flat surfaces and specialty sanding blocks on contours. When sanding hardwood, switch to 180-grit paper and sand again.

Raise the wood grain by dampening the surface with a wet rag. Let the wood dry, then skim the surface with a fine abrasive pad, following the grain.

Use sanding blocks to hand-sand the entire workpiece with the finest-grit paper in the sanding sequence. Sand until all sanding marks are gone and the surface is smooth. (Use bright sidelighting to check your progress.) If using sanding sealer, do that now.

How to Use Sanding Sealer

Make your own sanding sealer by blending one part clear topcoat material (not water-based) with one part topcoat solvent. *Note: Use the same topcoat material you plan to apply to the project.*

Wipe on a heavy coat of the sealer, then wipe off the excess after a few minutes. When dry, sand lightly with 220-grit sandpaper.

How to Apply Grain Filler

After finish sanding, use a rag or putty knife to spread a coat of grain filler onto the wood surface. With a polishing motion, work the filler into the grain. Let the filler dry until it becomes cloudy (usually about 5 minutes).

Remove excess filler by drawing a plastic scraper across the grain of the wood at a 45° angle. Let the grain filler dry overnight.

Lightly hand-sand the surface, following the direction of the grain, with 220-grit sandpaper. Finally, dampen a clean cloth with mineral spirits and use it to thoroughly clean the surface.

Installing Cabinets

Cabinets must be firmly anchored to wall studs, and they must be plumb and level when installed. The best way to ensure this is by attaching a ledger board to the wall to assist in the installation. As a general rule, install the upper cabinets first so your access is not impeded by the base cabinets. (Although some professionals prefer to install the base cabinets first so they can be used to support the uppers during installation.) It's also best to begin in a corner and work outward from there.

Stock cabinets are sold in boxes that are keyed to door and drawer packs (you need to buy these separately). It is important that you realize this when you are estimating your project costs at the building center (often a door pack will cost as much or more than the cabinet). Also allow plenty of time for assembling the cabinets out of the box. It can take an hour or more to put some more complex cabinets together.

Tools & Materials ▸

Handscrew clamps	Cabinets
Level	Trim molding
Hammer	Toe-kick molding
Utility knife	Filler strips
Nail set	Valance
Stepladder	6d finish nails
Drill	Finish washers
Counterbore drill bit	#10 × 4" wood screws
Cordless screwdriver	#8 × 2½" screws
Jig saw	3" drywall screws

How to Fit a Corner Cabinet

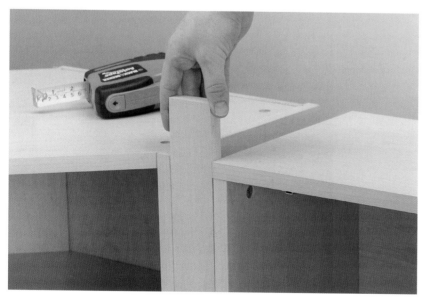

Before installation, test-fit corner and adjoining cabinets to make sure doors and handles do not interfere with each other. If necessary, increase the clearance by pulling the corner cabinet away from the side wall by no more than 4". To maintain even spacing between the edges of the doors and the cabinet corner, cut a filler strip and attach it to the corner cabinet or the adjoining cabinet. Filler strips should be made from material that matches the cabinet doors and face frames.

How to Install Wall Cabinets

1

Position a corner upper cabinet on a ledger and hold it in place, making sure it is resting cleanly on the ledger. Drill ³⁄₁₆" pilot holes into the wall studs through the hanging strips at the top, rear of cabinet. Attach the cabinet to the wall with 2½" screws. Do not tighten fully until all cabinets are hung.

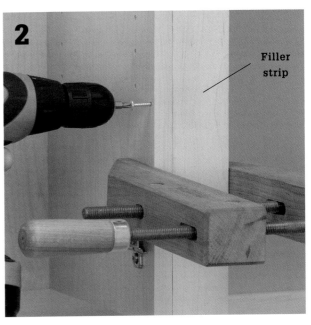

2

Filler strip

Attach a filler strip to the front edge of the cabinet, if needed. Clamp the filler in place, and drill counterbored pilot holes through the cabinet face frame, near hinge locations. Attach filler to cabinet with 2½" cabinet screws or flathead wood screws.

3

Position the adjoining cabinet on the ledger, tight against the corner cabinet or filler strip. Clamp the corner cabinet and the adjoining cabinet together at the top and bottom. Handscrew clamps will not damage wood face frames.

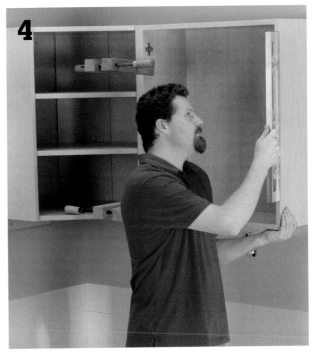

4

Check the front cabinet edges or face frames for plumb. Drill ³⁄₁₆" pilot holes into wall studs through hanging strips in rear of cabinet. Attach cabinet with 2½" screws. Do not tighten wall screws fully until all cabinets are hung.

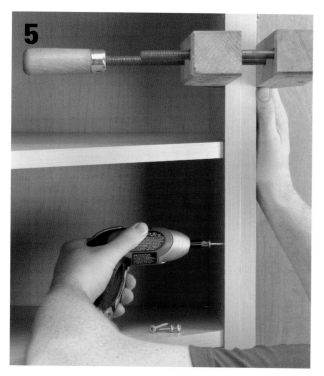

5

Attach the corner cabinet to the adjoining cabinet. From inside corner cabinet, drill pilot holes through face frame. Join cabinets with sheet-metal screws.

6

Position and attach each additional cabinet. Clamp frames together, and drill counterbored pilot holes through side of face frame. Join cabinets with wood screws. Drill 3/16" pilot holes in hanging strips, and attach cabinet to studs with wood screws.

7

Join frameless cabinets with #8 × 1¼" panhead wood screws or wood screws with decorative washers. Each pair of cabinets should be joined by at least four screws.

8

Fill gaps between the cabinet and wall or neighboring appliance with a filler strip. Cut the filler strip to fit the space, then wedge wood shims between the filler and the wall to create a friction fit that holds it in place temporarily. Drill counterbored pilot holes through the side of the cabinet (or the edge of the face frame) and attach filler with screws.

Remove the temporary ledger. Check the cabinet run for plumb, and adjust if necessary by placing wood shims behind cabinet, near stud locations. Tighten wall screws completely. Cut off shims with utility knife.

Use trim moldings to cover any gaps between cabinets and walls. Stain moldings to match cabinet finish.

Attach decorative valance above sink. Clamp valance to edge of cabinet frames, and drill counterbored pilot holes through cabinet frames into end of valance. Attach with sheet-metal screws.

Install the cabinet doors. If necessary, adjust the hinges so that the doors are straight and plumb.

How to Install Base Cabinets

Begin the installation with a corner cabinet. Draw plumb lines that intersect the 34½" reference line (measured from the high point of the floor) at the locations for the cabinet sides.

Place cabinet in corner. Make sure the cabinet is plumb and level. If necessary, adjust by driving wood shims under cabinet base. Be careful not to damage flooring. Drill ³⁄₁₆" pilot holes through the hanging strip and into wall studs. Tack the cabinet to the wall with wood screws or wallboard screws.

Clamp the adjoining cabinet to the corner cabinet. Make sure the new cabinet is plumb, then drill counterbored pilot holes through the cabinet sides or the face frame and filler strip. Screw the cabinets together. Drill ³⁄₁₆" pilot holes through hanging strips and into wall studs. Tack the cabinets loosely to the wall studs with wood screws or wallboard screws.

Use a jig saw to cut any cabinet openings needed in the cabinet backs (for example, in the sink base seen here) for plumbing, wiring or heating ducts.

Position and attach additional cabinets, making sure the frames are aligned and the cabinet tops are level. Clamp cabinets together, then attach the face frames or cabinet sides with screws driven into pilot holes. Tack the cabinets to the wall studs, but don't drive screws too tight—you may need to make adjustments once the entire bank is installed.

Make sure all cabinets are level. If necessary, adjust by driving shims underneath cabinets. Place shims behind the cabinets near stud locations to fill any gaps. Tighten wall screws. Cut off shims with utility knife.

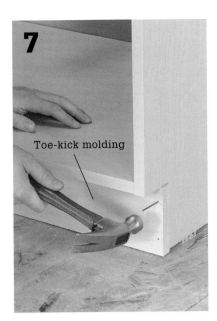

Toe-kick molding

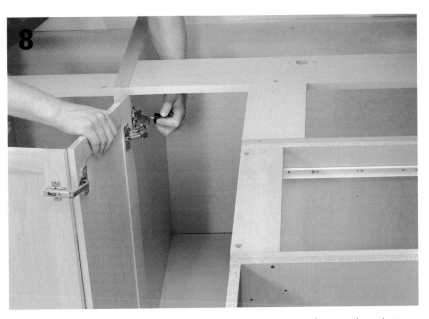

Use trim moldings to cover gaps between the cabinets and the wall or floor. The toe-kick area is often covered with a strip of wood finished to match the cabinets or painted black.

Hang cabinet doors and mount drawer fronts, then test to make sure they close smoothly and the doors fit evenly and flush. Self-closing cabinet hinges (by far the most common type installed today) have adjustment screws that allow you to make minor changes to the hardware to correct any problems.

Creating a Kitchen Island

Kitchen islands can be created using a whole range of methods, from repurposing an old table to fine, custom woodworking. But perhaps the easiest (and most failsafe) way to add the conveniences and conviviality of a kitchen island is to make one from stock base cabinets. The cabinets and countertops don't have to match your kitchen cabinetry, but that is certainly an option you should consider. When designing and positioning your new island, be sure to maintain a minimum distance of 3 ft. between the island and other cabinets (4 ft. or more is better).

Tools & Materials ▸

Marker
Drill/driver
2 × 4 cleats
Pneumatic nailer and
  2" finish nails or
  hammer and
  6d finish nails

2 base cabinets (approx.
  36" wide × 24" deep)
Countertop
Wallboard screws

Two base cabinets arranged back-to-back make a sturdy kitchen island base that's easy to install. When made with the same style cabinets and countertops as the rest of the kitchen, the island is a perfect match.

How to Create a Stock-cabinet Island

1

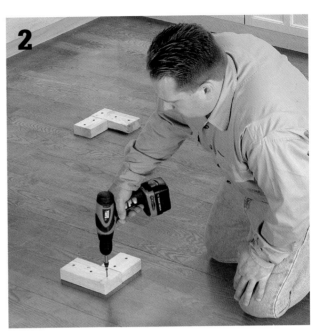

2

Set two base cabinets back-to-back in position on the floor and outline the cabinet corners onto the flooring. Remove the cabinets and draw a new outline inside the one you just created to allow for the thickness of the cabinet sides (usually ¾").

Cut 2 × 4 cleats to fit inside the inner outline to provide nailing surfaces for the cabinets. Attach the cleats to the floor with screws or nails. TIP: Create an L-shape cleat for each inside corner.

3

4

Join the two base cabinets together by driving 1¼" wallboard screws through the nailing strips on the backs of the cabinets from each direction. Make sure the cabinet sides are flush and aligned. Lower the base cabinets over the cleats. Check the cabinets for level, and shim underneath the edges of the base if necessary.

Attach the cabinets to the floor cleats using 6d finish nails. Drill pilot holes for nails, and recess nail heads with a nail set. Make a countertop and install it on top of the cabinets.

Making Countertops

More than simply a work surface, a kitchen countertop is an important part of many built-ins that can dazzle with the look-at-me pizzazz of granite, or bring together a country theme with soapstone and butcher block. There are many choices in countertops, from the less expensive laminate and post-form, through ceramic and stone tile, to high-end stainless-steel, granite and marble.

Countertop options for your built-in depend on how much you are willing to spend, whether you will be doing the work yourself or contracting out, and what look you want to achieve. In this chapter we will cover several countertop options, identifying their pluses and minuses, and giving installation directions for those you can install yourself.

Step-by-step instructions with photographs are included for two countertop projects: post-form laminated, custom laminate.

Butcher Block ▶

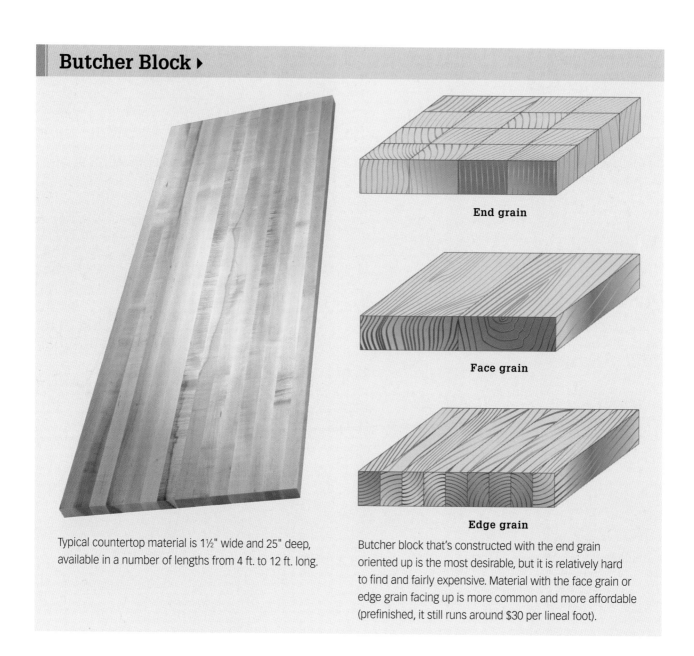

End grain

Face grain

Edge grain

Typical countertop material is 1½" wide and 25" deep, available in a number of lengths from 4 ft. to 12 ft. long.

Butcher block that's constructed with the end grain oriented up is the most desirable, but it is relatively hard to find and fairly expensive. Material with the face grain or edge grain facing up is more common and more affordable (prefinished, it still runs around $30 per lineal foot).

A well-chosen countertop can give your built-in a high-end appearance and a professional finish.

3

Hold the endcap laminate against the end, slightly overlapping the edges. Activate adhesive by pressing an iron set at medium heat against the endcap. Cool with a wet cloth, then file the endcap laminate flush with the edges of the countertop.

4

Position the countertop on base cabinets. Make sure the front edge of the countertop is parallel to the cabinet faces. Check the countertop for level. Make sure that drawers and doors open and close freely. If needed, adjust the countertop with shims.

5

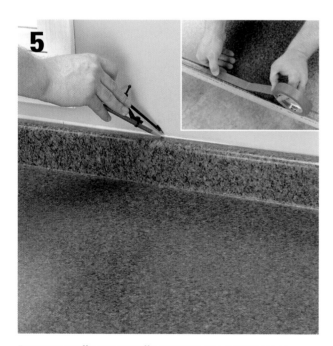

Because walls are usually uneven, use a compass to trace the wall outline onto the backsplash. Set the compass arms to match the widest gap, then move the compass along the length of the wall to transfer the outline to the top of the backsplash. Apply painter's tape to the top edge of the backsplash, following the scribe line (inset).

6

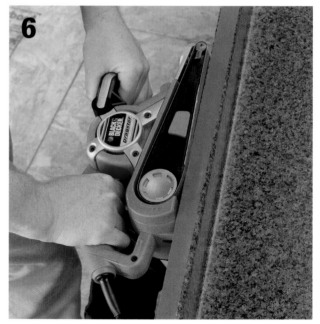

Remove the countertop. Use a belt sander to grind the backsplash to the scribe line. Replace and install the countertop.

Tips for Installing Post-form Countertops ▸

Mark the cutout for a self-rimming sink by tracing it. Position the sink upside down on the countertop and trace its outline. Remove the sink and draw a cutting line ⅝" inside the sink outline.

Drill a starter hole just inside the cutting line. Make sink cutouts with a jig saw. Support the cutout area from below so that the falling cutout does not damage the cabinet or countertop.

Apply a bead of silicone caulk to the edges of the mitered countertop sections. Force the countertop pieces tightly together.

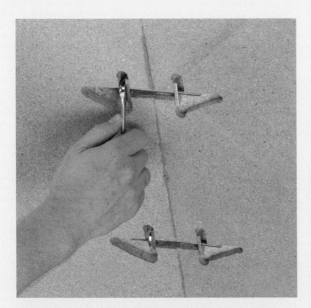

From underneath the countertop, install and tighten miter take-up bolts. Position the countertop tightly against the wall and fasten it to the cabinets by driving wallboard screws up through corner brackets and into the countertop. Screws should be long enough to provide maximum holding power, but not long enough to puncture the laminate surface.

Seal the seam between the backsplash and the wall with silicone caulk. Smooth the bead with a wet fingertip. Wipe away excess caulk.

How to Build a Custom Laminate Countertop

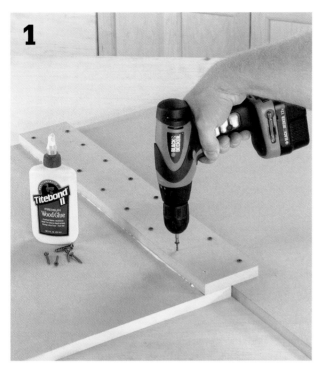

Join the countertop substrate pieces on the bottom side. Attach a 4" particleboard joint support across the seam, using carpenter's glue and 1¼" wallboard screws.

Attach 3"-wide edge buildup strips to the bottom of the countertop, using 1¼" wallboard screws. Fill any gaps on the outside edges with latex wood patch, and then sand the edges with a belt sander.

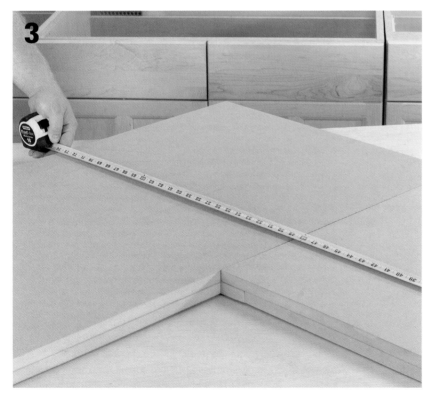

To determine the size of the laminate top, measure the countertop substrate. Laminate seams should not overlap the substrate. Add ½" trimming margin to both the length and width of each piece. Measure laminate needed for face and edges of backsplash, and for exposed edges of countertop substrate. Add ½" to each measurement.

4

Cut laminate by scoring and breaking it. Draw a cutting line, then etch along the line with a utility knife or other sharp cutting tool. Use a straightedge as a guide. Two passes of scoring tool will help laminate break cleanly.

OPTION: Some laminate installers prefer to cut laminate with special snips that resemble avaiator snips. Available from laminate suppliers, the snips are faster than scoring and snapping, and less likely to cause cracks or tears in the material. You'll still need to square the cut edges with a trimmer or router.

5

Bend laminate toward the scored line until the sheet breaks cleanly. For better control on narrow pieces, clamp a straightedge along the scored line before bending laminate. Wear gloves to avoid being cut by sharp edges.

6

Create tight-piloted seams with plastic laminate by using a router and a straight bit to trim edges that will butt together. Measure from cutting edge of the bit to edge of the router baseplate (A). Place laminate on scrap wood and align edges. To guide the router, clamp a straightedge on the laminate at distance A plus ¼", parallel to laminate edge. Trim laminate.

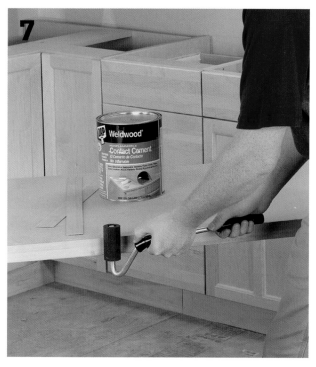

Apply laminate to sides of countertop first. Using a paint roller, apply two coats of contact cement to the edge of the countertop and one coat to back of laminate. Let cement dry according to manufacturer's directions. Position laminate carefully, then press against edge of countertop. Bond by rolling with a J-roller.

Use a router and flush-cutting bit to trim edge strip flush with top and bottom surfaces of countertop substrate. At edges where router cannot reach, trim excess laminate with a file. Apply laminate to remaining edges, and trim with router.

Test-fit laminate top on countertop substrate. Check that laminate overhangs all edges. At seam locations, draw a reference line on core where laminate edges will butt together. Remove laminate. Make sure all surfaces are free of dust, then apply one coat of contact cement to back of laminate and two coats to substrate. Place spacers made of ¼"-thick scrap wood at 6" intervals across countertop core. Because contact cement bonds instantly, spacers allow laminate to be positioned accurately over core without bonding. Align laminate with seam reference line. Beginning at one end, remove spacers and press laminate to countertop core.

Apply contact cement to remaining substrate and next piece of laminate. Let the cement dry, then position laminate on spacers, and carefully align the butt seam. Beginning at seam edge, remove spacers and press laminate to the countertop substrate.

Roll the entire surface with a J-roller to bond the laminate to the substrate. Clean off any excess contact cement with a soft cloth and mineral spirits.

Flush cutting bit

Remove excess laminate with a router and flush-cutting bit. At edges where router cannot reach, trim excess laminate with a file. Countertop is now ready for final trimming with bevel-cutting bit.

13

15° bevel-cutting bit

Finish-trim the edges with router and 15° bevel-cutting bit. Set bit depth so that the bevel edge is cut only on top laminate layer. Bit should not cut into vertical edge surface.

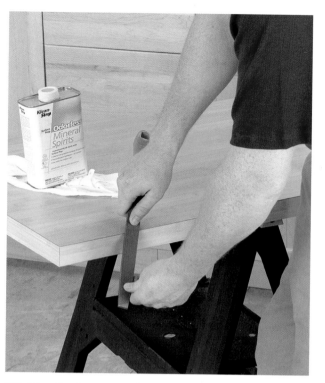

TIP: File all edges smooth. Use downward file strokes to avoid chipping the laminate.

14

Cut 1¼"-wide strips of ¼" plywood to form an overhanging scribing strip for the backsplash. Attach to the top and sides of the backsplash substrate with glue and wallboard screws. Cut laminate pieces and apply to exposed sides, top and front of backsplash. Trim each piece as it is applied.

15

Test-fit the countertop and backsplash. Because your walls may be uneven, use a compass to trace the wall outline onto the backsplash scribing strip. Use a belt sander to grind the backsplash to scribe line.

16

17

Apply a bead of silicone caulk to the bottom edge of the backsplash.

Position the backsplash on the countertop, and clamp it into place with bar clamps. Wipe away excess caulk, and let dry completely.

Screw 2" wallboard screws through the countertop and into the backsplash core. Make sure screw heads are countersunk completely for a tight fit against the base cabinet. Install countertops.

18

Creating Wood Countertop Edges

For an elegant added touch on a laminate countertop, use hardwood edges and shape them with a router. Rout the edges before attaching the backsplash to the countertop. Wood caps can also be added to the top edge of the backsplash. A simple edge is best for easy cleaning.

Tools & Materials ▸

Hammer
Nail set
Belt sander with 120-grit sanding belt
3-way clamps

Router
1 × 2 hardwood strips
Wood glue
Finish nails

Incorporating hardwood into the countertop edging presents a wealth of attractive and very durable solutions for the nosing of a plastic laminate countertop.

How to Build Solid Hardwood Edges

Apply laminate to the top of the countertop before attaching the edge strip. Attach the edge strip flush with the surface of the laminate, using wood glue and finish nails.

Mold the top and bottom edges of the strip with a router and profiling bit, if desired. Stain and finish the wood as desired.

How to Build Coved Hardwood Edges

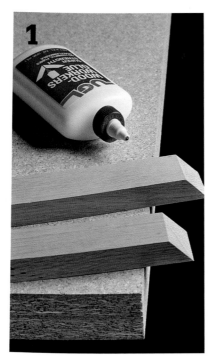

Cut 1 × 2 hardwood strips to fit the edges of the countertop. Sand the strips smooth. Miter-cut the inside and outside corners.

Attach edge strips to the countertop with wood glue and 3-way clamps. Drill pilot holes, then attach strip with finish nails. Recess nail heads with a nail set or, use a pneumatic finish nailer with 2" nails.

Sand the edge strips flush with the top surface of the countertop, using a belt sander and 120-grit sandpaper.

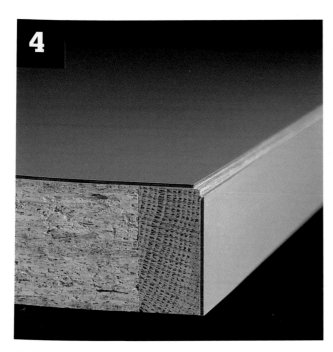

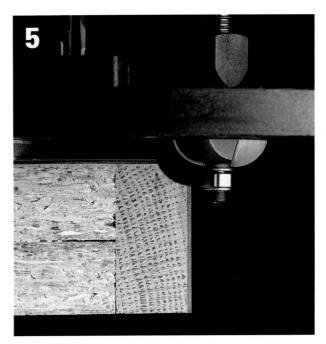

Apply laminate to the edge and top of the countertop after the hardwood edge has been sanded flush.

Cut cove edge with a router and cove bit with ball-bearing pilot. Smooth cove with 220-grit sandpaper. Stain and finish exposed wood as desired.

BUILT-IN PROJECTS

Window Seat

One great way to add cozy charm to a room is to build a window seat. Not only do window seats make a room more inviting, they provide functional benefits as well, particularly when you surround them with built-in shelving. The window seat shown here has a base built from above-the-refrigerator cabinets. This size provides just the right height (when placed on a 3" curb) to create a comfortable seat.

Above the cabinets and flanking each side is a site-made bookcase. A top shelf bridges the two cases and ties the whole thing together—while creating still more space for storage or display.

Tools

Miter saw
Table saw
Circular saw
Drill/driver
Level
Stud finder
Hammer
Tape measure
Nail set
Pneumatic nailer/compressor
Router
Shooting board
Sander
Framing square

Materials

2) 15" upper refrigerator
   cabinets
2) ¾" × 4 × 8 ft. pcs. MDF or
   plywood
Screws/nails
1) ¼" × 4 × 8 ft. lauan plywood
Caulk
Primer
Paint

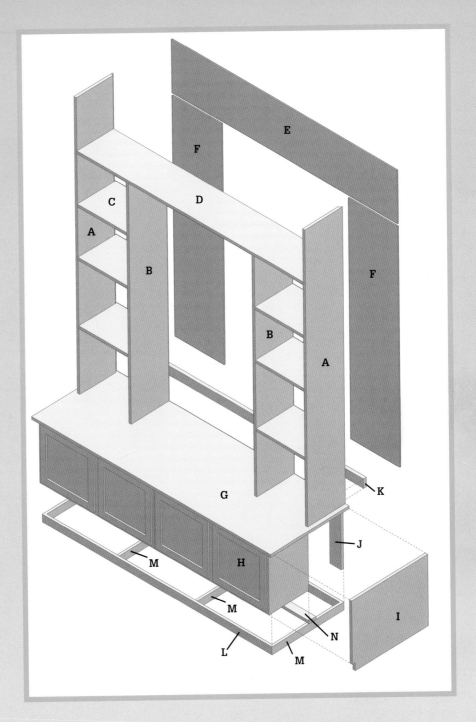

Cutting List

Part	No.	Desc.	Size	Material
A	2	Outer standard	¾ × 11½ × 77¼"	MDF
B	2	Inner standard	¾ × 11½ × 63¼"	MDF
C	6	Shelf	¾ × 16½ × 11¼"	MDF
D	1	Top shelf	¾ × 11¼ × 70½"	MDF
E	1	Top backer	¼ × 13¼ × 71⅜"	Plywood
F	2	Backers	¼ × 17½ × 63¼"	Plywood
G	1	Seatboard	¾ × 25 × 74"	MDF

Part	No.	Desc.	Size	Material
H	2	Bridge cabinets	15 h × 36" w	Stock cabinets
I	2	End panel	¾ × 24 × 18"	MDF
J	4	Nailer	¾ × 2½ × 15"	Plywood
K	1	Ledger	¾ × 2½ × 72"	Plywood
L	2	Curb rim	¾ × 3 × 72"	MDF
M	4	Curb strut	¾ × 3 × 22½"	MDF
N	1	Cabinet nailer	¾ × 3 × 72"	MDF

How to Build a Window Seat

The key control point for laying this project out is the center of the window sill. Measure and mark it.

After striking a level line at cabinet height, measure from the floor in three locations to make sure the cabinets will fit.

Strike a plumb line on each edge of the cabinet run. Use a 4-foot level and strike the line from floor to ceiling.

LAY OUT THE PROJECT

This window seat is integrated with the existing window and trimwork. The key control point for laying out the base cabinets is locating the center of the window opening. It is also important that the cabinets sit level both left-to-right and front-to-back. Level cabinet tops make installing the upper cabinet cases much easier.

Before you begin building, relocate or remove any electrical outlets that'll be covered by the cabinet, according to your local electrical codes. For example, you can't just dead-end wires and leave them buried in a wall. They usually need to be capped and placed in a junction box with a removable faceplate that is accessible (which may mean making a cutout in the back of a cabinet panel).

Mark the center of the window opening on the sill (photo 1). Use a square and a level to transfer that mark plumb down the wall to the cabinet height location. At the height of the cabinets mark a level line. Measure from the floor up to the level line in several locations to make sure the cabinets will fit all along their entire run (photo 2). If they don't fit, make the proper adjustments; that is, raise the line. Cabinets that don't come up to the line must be shimmed so they are level. Using an electronic stud finder, find and mark the wall stud locations beneath the window and on each side in the project area. *Note: You should find jack and king studs directly on either side of the window and a header above the window. Determine the overall span of the cabinets you choose. For the project shown here, the bank will be 6 ft. long, measuring from outside-edge to outside-edge. Use a level to mark the outside edges of the cabinet run on the wall. Mark plumb lines down to the floor and up to the ceiling (photo 3).*

INSTALL THE BASE CABINETS

With all the layout lines marked out, the next step is to install the cabinets that form the base of the window seat. This determines the control points for the rest of the project layout. Use a pull-saw and sharp chisel to remove base molding between the vertical layout lines (photo 4).

To elevate the cabinets that will be used for the seat to a more comfortable height, and to create a toe-kick space, build a short curb that matches the footprint of the seat. Since the curb will not be visible, you can use just about any shop scraps you may have to build it. The one shown here is made with MDF sheet stock that is rip-cut into 3"-wide strips. Then the curb is assembled into a ladder shape by attaching struts between the front and back curb members with glue and screws (photo 5). Once the ladder is built, set the cabinets on the curb so the cabinet fronts and sides align with the curb. Mark the location of the backs of the cabinets onto the top of the curb and then remove the cabinets. Attach a nailer to the curb just behind the line for the cabinet backs. Then, position the curb tight against the wall in the area where the base molding has been removed. Attach it to the sill plate of the wall with nails or screws.

To support the back edge of the seatboard, attach a ledger to the wall. The top of the ledger (we used a 2½"-wide strip of plywood) should be flush with the tops of the cabinets when they are installed on top of the curb. Attach the ledger with panel adhesive and nails or screws driven at stud locations (photo 6). Measure between the top of the curb and ledger and cut a few nailers to this length.

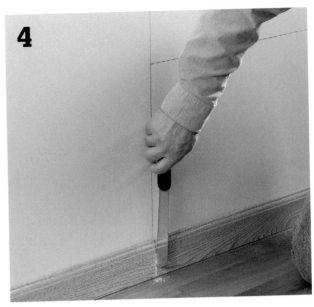

Because a pull-type saw requires almost zero clearance at the bottom of a cut (where it would hit the floor in this application), it's great for removing the base molding so the cabinet carcases fit tight to the wall.

Assemble the curb members into a ladder-like frame and secure the butt joints with glue and screws driven through pilot holes.

Attach a ledger for the back edge of the seatboard to the wall, using panel adhesive and screws or nails driven at stud locations.

7

Cut nailers to fit between the ledger and the curb and attach them to the wall at the ends of the project area.

8

For floors that are out of level, shim the cabinets up to the level line to keep them in a level plane.

9

After clamping the cabinet face-frames together, pre-drill and fasten them together with screws.

Attach them to the wall at the ends of the project, and add a couple near the center to help support the ledger (photo 7).

Set the cabinets in position on the curb, with the back edges against the nailer. Drive shims between the curb and the floor if necessary to level the cabinets (photo 8). Fasten the cabinets to the nailer strip. Pre-drill, countersink and face-fasten the face frames together with screws to form a "gang" of cabinets (photo 9). If you are using cabinets that have no face frames, screw the cabinet sides together as directed by the cabinet manufacturer. Cut off shims as necessary.

If the ends of your window seat are open (that is, they don't butt up against a wall), cut end panels to cover the ends of the cabinets and the open space behind them. Use ¼" plywood or hardboard. You may need to remove a sliver of the baseboard on each side so you can butt the panels up against the wall. Attach the panel to the cabinet ends and the curb with panel adhesive.

Cut, rout and install the seat top. Cutting a 74" × 25" blank from MDF (medium-density fiberboard) works well. This will create a one inch overhang at the front and sides of the cabinets.

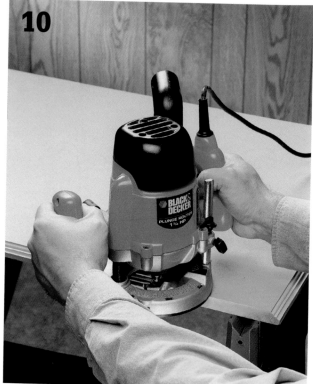

10

Before installing the seat top, rout a profile on the front and side edges. Don't rout the back.

Use a router and bit with a decorative profile (such as an ogee or a plain roundover) to smooth the hard edge of the MDF (photo 10). Profiling the edge reduces the chance that the edge will chip or crack. Position the seat top on top of the cabinets and the wall ledger and fasten it from the interior of the cabinets using coarse-threaded drywall screws. A bead of panel adhesive along the top edges of the cabinet and the ledger helps ensure a solid connection.

CUT THE CASE STOCK

The bookcase portion of the window seat can be assembled from sheet stock (MDF is a good choice) or solid 1× stock, such as 1 × 12 pine or poplar (pine is cheaper, poplar is stronger and takes paint better) or hardwood like maple, oak, or cherry for staining. Whatever material you choose, install a backer sheet of ¼" plywood that fits into rabbets in the backs of the case stock to help ensure square assembly and provide a strong connection point to the wall.

The actual width of 1 × 12 dimension lumber is 11½", so if using sheet stock, rip all pieces to width. Any edges that face the interior of the room need to be sanded smooth to remove saw marks. Note that it's usually easier to dress the factory edge than the edge cut on-site. Running the pieces on a jointer or router table is a fast, accurate way to dress the edge. A belt sander or finish sander with fine grit paper works too, but be careful not to remove too much stock. Of course, you can also hand sand it.

Cut a ½" wide by ¼" deep rabbet (see drawing, page 81) on the backs of the standards (photo 11). You can do this with a table saw (either make multiple passes on the table saw to remove stock or use a stacked dado head cutter blade); using a router with a rabbeting bit; or on a jointer or router table. The remainder of the layout and sizing must be registered from the seat top to accommodate specific site conditions.

INSTALL THE TOP-SHELF BACKER

The remaining measurements for the backer and shelf dimensions are now determined by the distance between your window casing, vertical layout lines, and ceiling height. They must be site-measured for accuracy.

Lay out the top shelf backer (photo 12). It should fit between the ceiling and the top of the window casing—and between your vertical layout lines. To calculate the top shelf backer dimensions, measure between the vertical layout lines. Subtract ⅝". To calculate top shelf backer height, measure from the top of the window casing to the ceiling. Subtract ⅛".

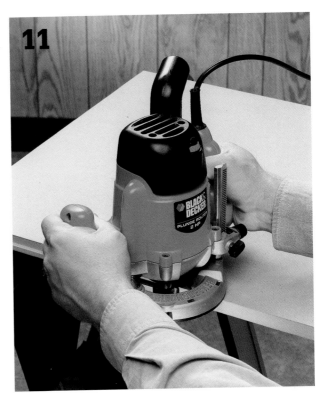

Clamp all work securely before milling the ½ × ¼ rabbet, for the backers with a router, which will provide safe, accurate cuts. The remainder of the layout and sizing must be registered from the seat top to accommodate specific site conditions.

Use the layout lines to size the top shelf backer and the backers for the vertical shelf units.

Marking layout lines all at once using a framing square is a good way to keep lines parallel from shelf-to-shelf. Make sure all bottoms are held flush during the marking procedure.

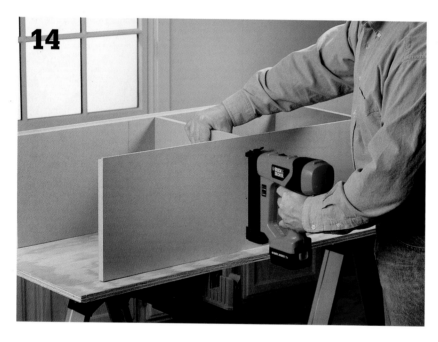

Install the rest of the shelves taking care to drive fasteners straight to prevent blow-outs in the shelf stock.

Install the top shelf backer tight to the ceiling by fastening to studs with finish nails or screws.

FABRICATE & ASSEMBLE THE BOOKCASES
The bookcases' outside edges run from the seat-top to the ceiling. The inside edges run from the seat-top to the top of the window casing. Measure and cut each vertical bookcase member to length. On a flat surface, lay all the bottoms of the bookcase members flush and mark out your shelves (photo 13). Use a framing square to mark them. Keep in mind there is a bottom

shelf that sits directly above the seat top. The top shelf is installed later.

Lay out and cut the backer stock. To calculate the width, measure the distance between the window casing and the vertical layout line, minus ½". To calculate the height, measure the distance from the seat top to the bottom edge of the top backer and subtract ⅛".

Assemble the cabinet sides and the backers. This is an ideal application for a pneumatic ¼" crown stapler, but it can also be done effectively by pre-drilling and

15

Hold the shelf assembly as tight as possible to the window trim, seat top and wall then fasten.

16

For paint grade units, caulk any gaps that appear to make shadow lines disappear. You can caulk the gap on paint grade shelves too. Be extra diligent in wiping down the material after caulking.

screwing, or by using a pneumatic finish nailer. Use a framing square as a reference to be sure the cabinet carcases are as square as possible during assembly. Measure, cut, and install shelves at the layout lines (photo 14). Fasten through the cabinet carcass into the shelves. Pre-drill and countersink if using screws.

INSTALL THE BOOK CASES & TOP SHELF

Butt the left bookcase to the window trim and fasten it to a wall stud with a few screws or nails driven through the backer (photo 15). Make sure the case

sits as tightly to the wall, seat top, and window trim as possible. Expect to make some on-site corrections as necessary to accommodate out-of-plumb walls or other imperfections. Slight gaps can be caulked later. Repeat for the right-side bookcase and then measure, cut and install the top shelf. If painting, caulk wherever necessary (photo 16). Fill exposed holes for nails and screws, then prime and paint or apply another finish of your choice. Make or buy a comfortable seat cushion. Finally, brew a cup of coffee, grab a good book, and get busy relaxing.

Bed Surround

Headboards aren't the only way to adorn the head of a bead. Indeed, it can be dressed not only with form but with terrific function. Combining cabinets of differing sizes and shapes provides both the finish to a bed—that is often the sole domain of the attractive but purely decorative headboard—and the utility of cabinets that double as both decoration and much needed storage.

The cabinets' clean, defined lines lend this Bed Surround a modern feel while the option for above-bed lighting creates the halo of a warm and calm space for starting and ending the day or tucking away for a quick nap.

Before getting started, determine if you want the option of cabinet-mounted lights. If so, rough-in the wires and switch(es) prior to installing the cabinets. Once the cabinets are on site, prep them before hanging by drilling the appropriate holes to accommodate the wires and house the light fixtures.

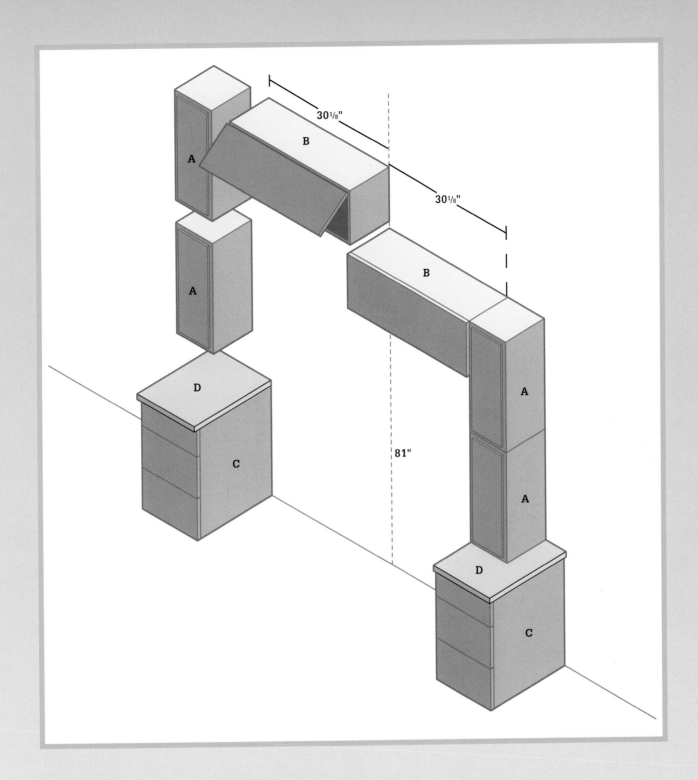

Cutting List

Part	No.	Desc.	Size
A	4	Wall cabinet	12 × 30"
B	2	Wall cabinet	15 × 30"
C	2	Base cabinet	18 × 34½"
D	2	Countertop	1½ × 19 × 25"

How to Build a Bed Surround

LAY OUT THE PROJECT

Choose the exact location for your bed surround. Mark the left and right edges of the project area, and then find the centerline. Be very exact. Using a 4 ft. level, plumb up from the center point. Mark a plumb line (photo 1). This is the control point from which you map out the rest of the layout. Measure 30⅛" left and right of the center point to mark the outside edges of the horizontal uppers (photo 2). Drive a 6-penny nail right on the centerline to hold your tape.

INSTALL THE UPPER CABINETS

Install a temporary ledger at the location of the bottom edges of the horizontal cabinets (81" above the floor in our project). Carefully install the horizontal uppers by resting them in position on the temporary ledgers and then driving screws through the cabinet backs and into wall studs (photo 3). If you discover gaps between upper cabinets, create filler strips to insert between the cabinets (photo 4) and conceal the gaps (see page 32).

From the outside edges of the installed horizontal upper assembly, plumb down to the floor with a 4-ft. level. With the uppers installed, you now have rock solid control points to plumb down to the floor from. These lines enable you to place the lower cabinets accurately and keep all face frames tight. Measure the base cabinets' width to the left and right of the plumb lines and mark the baseboard for removal (photo 5). Using a combination square and pull saw, mark and remove the base molding. Be careful not to damage the wallboard when removing the base molding.

INSTALL THE VERTICAL ELEMENTS

The base cabinets will need some type of countertop surface so they can function as nightstands and also support the vertical upper cabinets. We made particleboard countertops with plastic laminate applied to the tops and edges. Because the sizes are relatively small, this project also presents a good opportunity to experiment with some high-end countertop materials, such as granite or quartz. Install the countertops before installing the base cabinets in the project area (photo 6). Install the left base cabinet tight to the plumb line (photo 7).

Draw a plumb reference line in the exact center of the project area.

Mark vertical reference lines ⅛" further out from the centerline than the horizontal cabinet height.

3

Move the upper cabinets into position and fasten them to wall at stand locations using screws.

4

Cut and attach filler strips to the edge of one of the cabinets if there is a gap between it and its neighbor.

5

From the plumb line, measure out the exact width of the base cabinet carcass and mark the base molding for removal.

6

Install the laminate countertop on the base cabinet prior to installation. Make sure it is flush to the inside edge and back of the base cabinets and overhangs the front and outside edges.

7

Install the left base cabinet tight to the plumb line. Drive screws into a stud at both the top and bottom of the cabinet carcase.

On top of the left base cabinet, mount the first vertical upper tight to the plumb line. Be careful of the laminate countertop during installation. Mount the second vertical upper tight to the first. Make sure the face frames are flush. Shim the back as necessary and make sure to catch wall studs with the fasteners (photo 8). Repeat these steps for the base cabinet on the right side.

JOIN THE CABINETS

The horizontal uppers and vertical uppers should be at the same height. If so, flush up and fasten the face frames (photo 9).

If the cabinet gangs are not flush, adjust the horizontal uppers to mate with the left and right vertical gangs. Once flush in all directions, fasten the face frames and secure to the wall (photo 10).

Install (or have installed) the light fixtures and switches. Remove the temporary ledger, patch drywall, caulk, and trim cabinet bases as required. Sand and spot-touch the finishes.

Sometimes shims are required to keep face frames tight and flush, due to irregularities in the wall surface. Insert shims behind the cabinets as needed and remove excess shim material after installation.

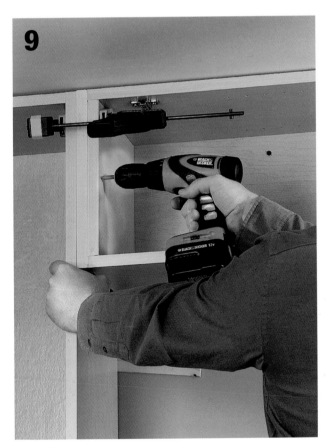

Fasten the face frames of the vertical uppers to the horizontal uppers. Pre-drill and countersink before driving screws.

Once the face frames are fastened together, attach the wall cabinets securely to the wall with screws driven through the cabinet backs at stud locations.

Loft Bed

If you had—or wanted—a loft bed back in college or in your first apartment, then this is a project you're going to like. But your kids will probably like it more because it's cool, fun, and their friends probably won't have one.

This loft bed is designed to open up floor space usually consumed by a bed. It also provides a location underneath it for a kid or kids to play, do activities or set up a desk. And, it because it ties in with the wall, it can work for kids of all ages.

Because you can tie into the wall, this loft bed probably has a little more oomph than the one you might have built with your old roommate. And, a built-in safety rail adds an extra layer of protection for younger kids. While you can make the bed to your own specifications following the techniques below, the bed design here is based on a twin-sized mattress, which is 39" × 75".

The outside dimensions of the bed frame are 48¾" × 80", which allows room up top for books, a drink, and a little extra room for the bedding to drape when the bed is made. Your little princess or prince will love climbing the ladder to get in bed.

Safety Note: Never attach hooks or handles to the loft bed and do not hang items from it, including rope and belts. Children can catch themselves on these items when playing or in the event that an accidental fall occurs.

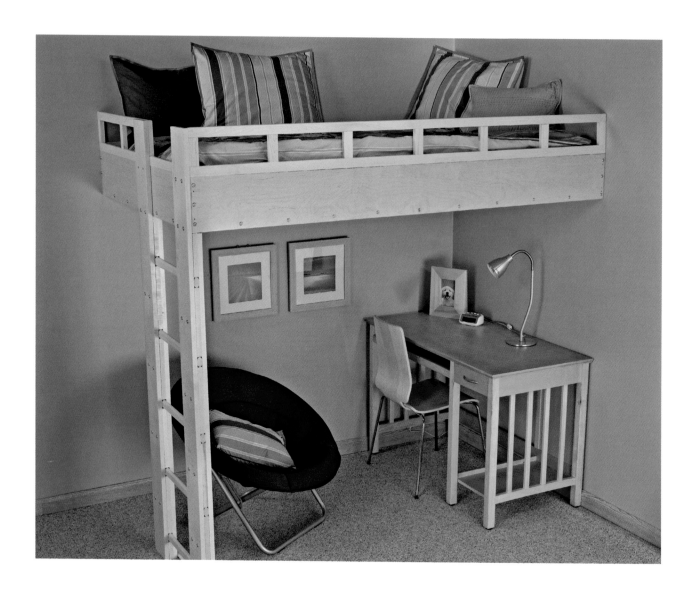

Tools

Miter saw
Table saw
Circular saw
Drill/driver
Level
Stud finder
Hammer
Tape measure
Nail set
Pneumatic nailer/compressor
Router and bits
Sander
Carpenter's square
Shooting board or straightedge

Materials

(2) ¾" × 4 × 8 ft. maple plywood
(6) 1 × 2 × 8 ft. maple
(4) 1 × 6 × 8 ft. maple
(3) 2 × 2 × 8 ft. pine
Brass screws
   with grommet washers
Deck screws
Trim head wood screws
Finishing materials

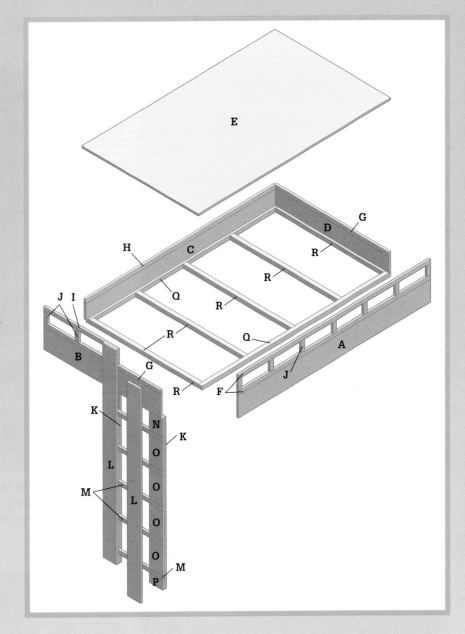

Cutting List

Part	No.	Desc.	Size	Material
A	1	Box front	¾ × 8 × 80"	Maple plywood
B	1	Box end–left	¾ × 8 × 48"	Maple plywood
C	1	Box back	¾ × 5¾ × 78½"	Maple plywood
D	1	Box end–right	¾ × 5¾ × 48	Maple plywood
E	1	Box bottom	¾ × 48 × 80"	Maple plywood
F	2	Box/rail cap–front	¾ × 1½ × 80"	1 × 2 maple
G	2	Box cap–end	¾ × 1½ × 48"	1 × 2 maple
H	1	Box cap–back	¾ × 1½ × 78½	1 × 2 maple
I	1	Rail cap–end	¾ × 1½ × 30¼	1 × 2 maple

Part	No.	Desc.	Size	Material
J	10	Rail post	¾ × 1½ × 4	1 × 2 maple
K	2	Ladder leg–short	¾ × 5½ × 59½"	1 × 6 maple
L	2	Ladder leg–long	¾ × 5½ × 79¼"	1 × 6 maple
M	6	Ladder rung	¾ × 1½ × 24	1 × 2 maple
N	2	Ladder filler	¾ × 5½ × 6½"	1 × 6 maple
O	8	Ladder filler	¾ × 5½ × 10½"	1 × 6 maple
P	2	Ladder filler	¾ × 5½ × 3½	1 × 6 maple
Q	2	Cleat–long	1½ × 1½ × 79¼	2 × 2 maple (or pine)
R	5	Cleat–short	1½ × 1½ × 45	2 × 2 maple (or pine)

Run the top edges of the 1 × 2 maple stock for the railing and edge caps parts through a router table fitted with a ¼" roundover bit. Cut the box caps, cap rails and rail posts to length (use a stop block on your power miter saw to make uniform length pieces). Attach the 1 × 2 caps to the back edge and right end (the wall sides) with glue and finish nails (drill pilot hole for the finish nails if hand-driving them). Before attaching the front and left side box caps, lay out positions for the railing posts according to the diagram on page 95 (photo 6). For best accuracy, gang-mark the post locations on the rail caps and box caps.

Attach each post to the box caps at marked locations, using glue and two 3" deck screws or wood screws driven up through pilot holes in the box

cap and into the bottom ends of the posts. Then, attach the box caps with attached posts to the front and left sides of the mattress box, using glue and 3" trim-head wood screws driven down through the top edges of the box caps and into the box at 12" intervals (photo 7).

Next, attach the railing caps to the tops of the railing posts with glue and trimhead wood screws driven down through the rail caps and into the posts. Make sure the posts are aligned with the reference lines you marked for their positions. Finish-sand the mattress box (you may want to back out the screws a ways to get underneath the grommets). It's best to wait until all parts are built so you can apply finish at the same time

Lay out the locations for the railing posts on the mating rail and box caps so you'll be sure they're aligned perfectly.

After screwing the railing posts to the box caps, attach the assemblies to the front and left sides of the mattress box using counterbored trim-head wood screws.

Shape the bullnose profiles into the top edges of your 1 × 2 rung stock before cutting the rungs to length.

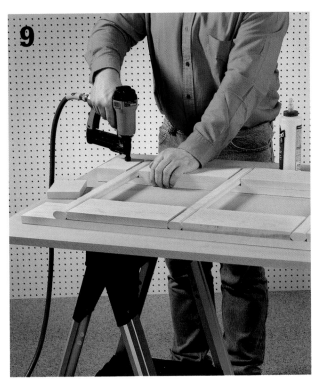

The ladder is a 3-ply assembly. The short leg is the first layer. Next come the ladder blocks that run parallel to the leg. After you install a ladder block, you install a rung perpendicular to it, working your way down the ladder—block, rung, block, rung, etc. Make sure the blocks are flush to the edges of the leg and that the rungs are held tight to the blocks. Use glue and screws (or pneumatic nails).

Adding a Ceiling ▶

The bottom edges of the front side and left end of the mattress box are still exposed plywood edge grain. There are a couple of ways of dealing with this. One is to conceal the edges with heat-activated maple veneer tape. Or, you can tack on additional strips of maple 1 × 2. But we chose to create a "ceiling" for the area underneath the loft bed by attaching a sheet of tempered ¼" hardboard to the underside of the box.

MAKE THE LADDER

The ladder/post is made from built-up 1 × 6 maple boards. The rungs are 1 × 2 maple boards with bull-nosed edges. To simplify the machining, cut the bullnoses by profiling all four edges of your 8-ft. 1 × 2 stock on a router table fitted with a ⅜" roundover bit (photo 8). The rungs should have a more pronounced bullnose than the top of the 1 × 2 box caps. Then cut the rungs to length with a miter saw or power miter saw (a stop block is a good idea for ensuring uniform lengths).

Cut the ladder legs and ladder blocks to length from 1 × 6 maple stock. Arrange the shorter legs on a flat surface with the outside edges 24" apart and the end flush. Make sure legs stay parallel at all times. Install the 6½" blocks first flush with the top ends of the legs. Use glue and a couple of finish nails or pneumatic nails to secure the blocks. Then begin working downward, adding rungs and blocks according to the diagram on page 95 (photo 9).

10

Attach the long outer legs to the blocks, rungs and short legs, ensuring that the bottoms and sides are flush. Glue and screw securely with flat head brass wood screws and decorative grommet-type washers.

Fasten the longer legs over the assembly, sandwiching the blocks and rung ends between 1 × 6 legs (photo 10). The extra 15" of length should be at the top of the longer legs.

INSTALL THE LOFT BED

Before installing the loft bed, apply your finish of choice (a few coats of durable polyurethane varnish is a good option). Pre-assemble the long side cleat and short side cleat into an L-shape, using glue and 3" deck screws. Attach the cleat to the wall at the mattress box layout lines. Apply panel adhesive to the back faces of the cleats before installing. Attach with $\frac{3}{8} \times 3\frac{1}{2}$" countersunk lag screws with washer at each stud location (photo 11).

Clamp a long 2 × 4 to the front face of the mattress box so the 2 × 4 will support the front at roughly the correct height when it is installed. With a couple of helpers (or more), raise the box and rest the back and right end on the walls cleats, making sure the box is square to the corners and flush against the walls. Place a level on the box and adjust the clamp and 2 × 4 brace so the box is level (photo 12).

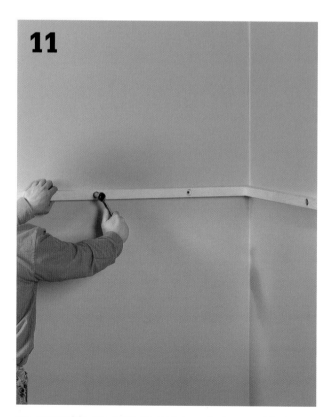

11

Pre-assemble the wall cleats into an L-shape and fasten them to the wall studs with lag screws and adhesive.

12

Check with a 4 ft. level across the corner of the box near the ladder location to make sure the box is level on both sides.

Position the ladder at the corner of the front and left side edges. The rung layer and short leg layer should fit snugly underneath the box, since the ladder will serve as a corner support post. Attach the ladder to the mattress box.

Secure the bottom of the ladder/corner post by attaching a cleat to the floor behind the ladder legs.

Once the mattress box is level, face-nail through the front and left ends of the box and into the wall cleats to hold the bed in place. After the ladder is secured and attached to the bed it will be safe enough to go topside and drive some nails through the box bottom and into the wall cleats.

INSTALL THE LADDER

Position the ladder under the mattress support box. Make sure that the right side of the ladder is flush with the long, outside edge of the mattress support box. Plumb it and fasten using glue and screws. The short legs of the ladder create a ledge to help support the free end of the box.

Drive 3½" brass screws with grommet washers through the ladder leg and upper ladder block at 8" intervals to secure the ladder (which functions as a post) to the mattress box (photo 13). Locate the screws so they hit the 2 × 2 cleat at the bottom, inside edge of the box. Also drive a few countersunk 2" screws down through the plywood box bottom and into the top ends of the short legs.

Double-check the ladder to make sure it is plumb and then screw the sixth ladder rung to the floor, directly behind the bottom of the ladder, laying flat (photo 14). The ends of the rungs should be flush with the outside faces of the ladder legs. Drive screws or nails through the rungs and into the bottoms of the legs to prevent the ladder from moving. Also attach the top ends of the long ladder legs to the top railing caps with trim-head screws. Drive a few extra nails through the box bottom and into the cleats, remove the temporary 2 × 4 brace, and add your mattress.

ADD THE BENCH BACKS

The backs of the benches are made by installing a plywood back board between the uprights and then cladding the backboard on both faces with tongue-and-groove paneling. Start by cutting the cleat that you'll use to anchor the back board from 1× stock. Cut eight cleats (4 for each bench) to 18" and cut four to 2¼". Install a short cleat and a long cleat in an L-shape on the inside face of each upright (photo 5). The top of the long cleat should be flush with the top of the upright.

Using a table saw or a circular saw and shooting board, cut the back panels to size. Apply a bead of wood glue or adhesive and lay the panels into the L-shaped brackets created by the two cleats (photo 6). Drive countersunk 1¼" screws through the back panel and into the long cleat. Install the remaining trim pieces around the plywood seat backer.

CLAD THE BENCHES

The bases and backs of the benches are clad with pine tongue-and-groove paneling (sometimes called carsiding). Because the paneling on the ends of the benches that face the room conceals their edges, install the paneling that's attached to the bench

Fabricate an L-shape to accept the plywood bench back, then attach it to a bench upright.

A plywood backer gives the bench back its rigidity. Install the backer using adhesive and fasteners.

along its length first. Cut the first paneling board to length so the bottom end is slightly above the floor and the top ends are flush with the tops of the bench supports (the top ends will be concealed by the seatboard overhang). Then, trim off the groove to create a solid wood edge at the end of the bench. If you own a pneumatic nailer, use it to drive nails through the tongue of the first paneling board. Otherwise, hand-nail with 4d or 6d finish nails and set the heads with a nail set. Drive at least one nail into each strut that the paneling board is positioned over (photo 7).

Apply paneling to the front and back of the bench base. To clad the bench ends (you only need to clad the end that will face the room), hold a paneling board up against the end and trace the angled edge onto the back side of the paneling (photo 8). Cut along this line. Install this piece flush to the bench end. Fasten and complete paneling installation for the bench base. Also install tongue-and-groove paneling boards on the front and back sides of each back panel. The boards should be flush with the top and bottom of the plywood back panel.

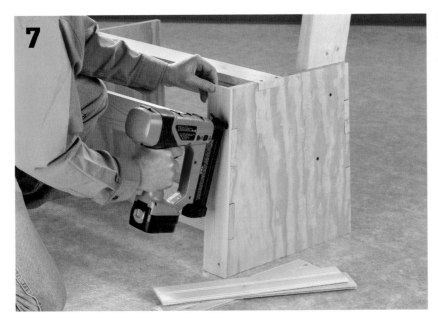

Begin installing the tongue-and-groove cladding on the base of the bench. You'll find many options, but ⅜"-thick paneling (sold in 14 sq. ft. packages) is an economical choice.

Trace the angle of the tapered bench onto the back side of a piece of paneling and trim it to fit.

13

Cut two identical leg halves, then trim 3" off the back one and face glue it with the front half to make a laminated table leg.

14

Attach the ledger for the tabletop to the wall with heavy-duty fasteners, such as counterbored lag screws driven at stud locations.

MAKE & INSTALL THE TABLE

The Country Diner table is designed to be affixed to a wall, supported by a ledger board on the wall side while a leg runs to the floor on the entry side. The length and width of the table are adjustable to suit your particular set-up but the fabrication techniques are the same. The dimensions specified in the drawing are 30" wide and 5 ft. long. The top of the table surface is 30" above the floor. Struts cut from 2 × 4 pine are added beneath the table for both looks and stability. We chose to glue up a rustic pine tabletop (which should get many coats of polyurethane varnish). You may prefer to have a tabletop fabricated from solid-surfacing, quartz or natural stone.

Lay out and cut the leg from 1 × 12 pine. The front half of the face-glued leg should run full height

(29¼"), tapering from 4" at the top to the full width of the 1 × 12 (11¼") at the bottom. Make the back half-of the laminated leg identical to the front, but then trim off the top 3" to create a ledge for the front tabletop strut (photo 13). Attach the ledgers (photo 14).

Rip-cut 2 × 4 pine stock to 3" wide to make all four tabletop struts. Also rip-cut some 1 × 4 stock for the two aprons. Cut the front strut to 28" long and then clip the bottom corners to give the table both some "lift" and to create leg room as you enter the booth. Cut the ledger and the inner struts to 24" long. Also cut the aprons to 52¼" long from the 1 × 4 stock. Locate exactly where your table will be fastened to your wall by arranging the location of your benches and then centering the table between them. Using a cardboard cut-out to tailor exactly where you want the

15

Assemble the table frame all at once on a flat surface.

16

Clamp the table leg to the front strut temporarily and check the tabletop for level. Attach the leg to the strut with glue and screws.

table and benches also will help you customize your diner. Once you find the center of the table location, find the center of the ledger board and mark it. When installing the ledger board, line up these two marks for a perfect fit. At the ledger board location, strike a level line 29¼" above the floor. Find and mark the wall stud locations—try to locate the ledger so it spans two studs. Install the ledger on layout using glue and the proper fasteners (photo 14). Ideally, use a ⅜" × 3½" counterbored lag screw driver through the ledger and into wall studs, plus additional screws and/or toggles to stabilize the ledger.

On a flat surface, assemble the table frame by capturing the short struts between the aprons (photo 15). The front strut should be attached to the aprons with L-brackets on the inside joint.

Attach the tabletop to the struts with one tabletop clip near each end of each strut. Clamp the leg to the front strut and rest the other end of the tabletop on the wall ledger, which should fit between the free ends of the aprons (photo 16). Adjust the height of the leg if necessary, and then attach it to the front strut with glue and screws. Drive screws through the aprons into the ends of the ledger.

APPLY FINISH, POUR COFFEE

The Country Diner is shown here with a light wood stain and high gloss polyurethane finish for ease of cleaning. Let all adhesives, finish and paint dry thoroughly before sitting down at the Country Diner for a slow home-cooked breakfast and time well spent with family and friends.

6

Measure and cut the inner end panel ½" shorter than the distance between the top plate and sole plate cross braces, and slide it in place. Align the panel with the edges of the top plate and sole plate cross braces, then attach it to the wall with 2½" screws driven into wall studs or blocking.

7

Planned height of countertop

1½"

Measure and cut plywood cabinet risers with holes for shelf supports (see Project Details, page 120). Risers should be ¼" narrower than end panels, and 1½" shorter than the distance from sole plate cross braces to planned countertop height. Attach a riser to each end panel, flush with the front edge, by driving 1¼" screws through counterbored pilot holes.

8

Cabinet riser

End panel

Base panel

¼" recess for back panel

Measure and cut plywood base panels the same width as the risers. Lay one base panel across the sole plate cross braces, butted against the riser at the inner end panel, with the ¼" recess at the back side (inset). Attach the base panel, using 2" finish nails.

9

Make riser assemblies (for inner riser locations) by joining two risers together, back-to-back, with glue and 1¼" finish nails. Set one riser assembly on the cross brace next to the first base panel, and attach it with 2½" screws driven through pilot holes and into the base panel edge.

Install the middle base panel, then the second riser assembly, then the last base panel, using the techniques shown in steps 8 to 9.

Measure and cut two plywood countertop panels, 24" wide, to fit between the end panels and set the first panel on the cabinet risers, flush with the front edges of the end panels. Use a framing square to adjust the risers so they are perpendicular to the countertop, then drill pilot holes and drive 2½" screws through countertop and into risers.

Apply glue to the top of the first countertop panel, then set the second countertop panel on the first panel. Clamp the panels together, then join them by driving 1" screws up through the underside of the first panel.

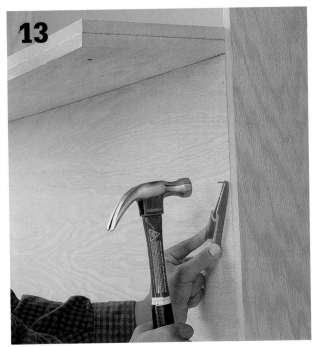

Measure and cut a ¼" oak plywood back panel to fit into the recess created by the back edges of the risers and base panels (see step 8). Set the back panel into the recess, then attach it to the cabinet risers and base panels, using 1" wire nails driven at 8" intervals.

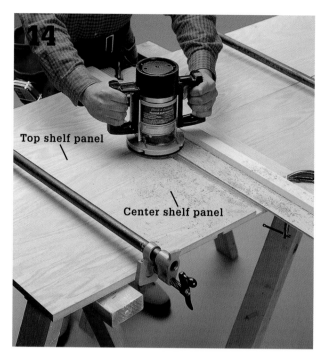

Measure and cut plywood shelf panels for the upper shelf unit, then cut ¾"-wide, ⅜"-deep dadoes at shelf riser locations (see Project Details, page 120). Tip: "Gang-cut" dadoes to speed up your work: mark locations for dado cuts on panels, then clamp them together so dado marks align.

Measure and cut plywood shelf unit sides. Make a ¾"-wide, ⅜"-deep dado in each side, where the center shelf panel will fit.

Measure and cut plywood shelf unit risers the same width as the center shelf. Stand the center shelf panel on its side, then glue the shelf risers into dadoes. Reinforce the joints with 2" screws driven into counterbored pilot holes.

Assemble the remaining pieces of the upper shelf unit, using glue and 2" screws driven into counterbored pilot holes. Attach side panels to center shelf, then attach top and bottom shelf panels to side panel and shelf risers. Make sure diagonal measurements of shelf unit are equal (if not, adjust unit as needed until it is square).

Measure and cut plywood shelf unit supports. Supports should be tall enough to leave a gap of about 1" beneath the top plates when the shelf unit is mounted on their top edges. Attach the shelf unit supports to the inner and outer end panels, using glue and 1¼" finish nails.

With a helper, lift the shelf unit onto the tops of the shelf unit supports. There should be a gap of about 1" between the shelf unit and the top plates.

Align the edges of the upper shelf unit with the edges of the end panels. Attach the shelf unit by driving 1¼" finish nails through the side panels and into the end panels. Space nails 4" apart, along outer edges of shelf unit.

Set a 2 × 4 brace between the countertop and the shelf unit, then measure and cut 1 × 4 top and bottom rails for the face frames. Miter the corner joints at the edges of the outer end panel, and butt the trim against the wall at the inner end panel. Drill pilot holes, and attach rails with glue and 2" finish nails driven into panels and framing members.

Measure and cut 1 × 4 countertop rail to reach from the wall to the outside edge of the outer end panel, on the front side of the room divider. Attach the rail to the edge of the countertop, using glue and 2" finish nails driven through pilot holes.

Measure and cut 1 × 2 face frame stiles to fit between the bottom rail and the top rail at the back of the room divider. Make a ¾" × 1½" notch in each stile, where the edge of the countertop will fit. Attach the stiles to the end panels, using glue and 2" finish nails driven through pilot holes.

Measure and cut 1 × 2 stiles to fit between the countertop rail and the top rail at the front of the room divider. Position stiles over the edges of the end panel, and attach with glue and 2" finish nails driven through pilot holes.

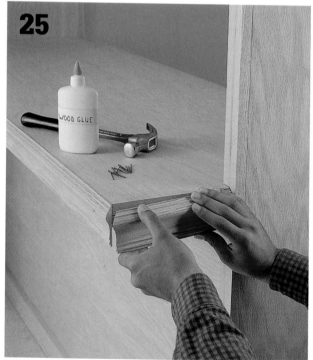

Cover the countertop overhang with ornamental trim molding mitered at a 45° angle at corner joints. Attach with glue and 1½" finish nails driven through pilot holes.

26

Measure and cut 1 × 3 stiles to fit between the bottom rail and the countertop rail on the back side of the room divider. Position end stiles flush with the outside faces of the end panels, and center the interior stiles over the riser assemblies. Attach with glue and 2" finish nails driven through pilot holes.

27

Attach ¾" shelf-edge strips to all exposed edges of the upper shelf unit, using glue and 1" finish nails driven through pilot holes. Cut horizontal strips the full length of the shelf unit, then add vertical strips between the horizontal strips.

28

Cut adjustable shelves for the cabinets, attach shelf-edge trim if desired, then install shelves, using pin-style shelf supports.

29

Cover gaps at ceiling with cove molding, and along floor and wall with base shoe molding. Fill holes, sand, then apply finish. Build, finish, and hang overlay cabinet doors (pages 46 to 47). Attach all remaining hardware.

How to Build a Laundry Center

Attach the base plate for the stub wall perpendicular to the wall, allowing space between the stub wall and the corner for your base cabinet.

After toe-nailing the studs to the base plate (and facenailing the stud next to the wall if possible) attach the cap plate, making sure the studs are vertical.

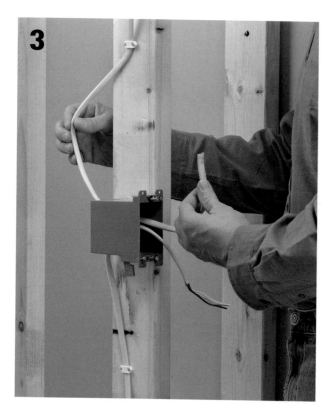

Run cable and install boxes for the light fixtures. Hire an electrician to do this if you are not experienced with home wiring. (Note that you will need to apply for a permit and have your wiring inspected.)

FRAME THE STUB WALL

This built-in laundry center is anchored by a 7-foot-tall, 24"-wide stub wall, so start by framing the wall. Measure out from the corner the width of your base cabinet (36" here) and draw a 24"-long reference line perpendicular to the wall. Cut a 2 × 4 wall plate to 24" and attach it to the floor. If you are building in a basement with a concrete floor, use pressure-treated lumber for the base plate and attach it by driving concrete nails with a powder-actuated nailer (photo 1).

Cut three 2 × 4s to 79" long and attach them to the base plate by toe-nailing (reinforce connections with L-brackets if you wish). Then, cut a 24"-long cap plate and nail it to the free ends of the studs with 16d common nails (photo 2). If you are installing overhead lighting, run cable from the power source (don't hook up the wires yet) through the studs and to an electrical switch box mounted to the wall frame (photo 3). Also run sheathed cable from the electrical box and out through a hole in the wall cap plate. Run enough cable to reach the light fixtures. We wired the fixtures in series: the power lead goes to the electrical box for the undercabinet light first, and then runs from the box to the canister light. If you prefer to switch the light independently, install a double gang box and cable for two switched circuits.

INSTALL THE BASE CABINET

We designed this laundry center with matching base and upper cabinets. Install the base cabinet between the stub wall and the corner (photo 4—see pages 58 to 59 for information on installing base cabinets). You can use just about any type of countertop material you wish. We selected maple butcher block because it can resist water and heat, requires very little maintenance, and makes a nice surface for folding laundry. Plus, it matches the maple cabinets and trim boards. To secure butcher block, you need to drill extra-large guide holes through the nailing strips on the base cabinet and attach the countertop with a short screws and washers (photo 5). This allows the material to move as it expands and contracts, which butcher block will do.

INSTALL THE WALLS

At the very least, you'll need to cover both sides of the stub wall for your laundry center. If the walls in your installation area are fit for covering with tileboard, you won't need to create any additional wall surfaces. In part to create an attachment surface for the clothes rod, we also installed a wall surface on the left side of the project area. The wall surfaces are created by attaching sheathing to the wall studs and then bonding water-resistant tileboard over the faces of the sheathing with panel adhesive. Cut a piece of wall sheathing that's the same width as the stub wall and reaches the same height when placed on the countertop surface. Attach the sheathing to the side of the countertop

Install the base cabinet between the stub wall and the corner, making sure it is level and securely attached to at least one wall.

Attach the countertop material (butcher block is seen here). The countertop should be flush against both walls and it should overhang the base cabinet slightly.

Mount the hardware and box for the light fixture to the ceiling panel before you install the ceiling.

Attach the ceiling panel to the laundry center wall and the cabinets.

Make the wiring connections at the light fixtures (left) and at the switch (right).

Attach tileboard to the ceiling panel on the face that will be facing downward. Then, plot out the locations for the light fixtures and mount the housings and ceiling boxes to the back of the ceiling panel as needed (photo 11). Set the ceiling panel over the laundry center and attach it with nails or screws driven into the top plate of the stub wall and the cabinet sides (photo 12).

HOOK UP LIGHTS & INSTALL TRIM

Make the wiring connections at the light fixtures and at the switch (photos 13a and 13b). You will need to have a wiring inspection before making the final hookup at the power source.

Cut pieces of 1 × 6" maple to make the top trim. Miter the outside and inside corners as you install the trim. Use a pneumatic nailer to attach the trim if you have access to one (photo 14). Attach the vertical trim members to cover the wall at the left side of the project and the end of the stub wall (photo 15). Scribe as necessary (see page 66) and rip the stub wall trim to fit. For a more finished look, round over the edges of the vertical trim pieces slightly.

Finally, slide in, level and hook up your washer and dryer (photo 16). Make sure to follow local codes for water and drain supply and for venting your dryer.

Trim out the top of the structure with 1 × 4 hardwood to conceal the gap beneath the ceiling panel. If you prefer, you can use crown molding here.

Attach the vertical trim boards, butting them up against the top trim and keeping the bottom slightly above the floor. Apply a finish and top coat to the trim boards as desired.

Install your washer and dryer (or have your appliance dealer install them for you).

How to Build a Towel Tower

INSTALL THE BASE CABINETS

Begin by making the seatboard that tops the refrigerator cabinet. Cut a piece of medium density fiberboard (MDF) so it is 1" wider than the cabinet and a couple of inches longer front-to-back (make it about 26" if using a 24" cabinet as shown here). Mount a piloted ogee or roundover bit (or other profiling bit of your choice) into your router and shape the front and side edges (photo 1). You'll probably get a little bit of blow-out at the back edge, which is why it's recommended that you make the workpiece a couple of inches too long. Once you've routed the profiles, trim the back edge so the front overhangs the cabinet by 1". Coat all faces and edges with primer and at least two coats of paint.

Attach the seatboard with screws driven through the mounting strips on the cabinet top and into the underside of the seatboard. The back edge of the seatboard should be flush with the back edge of the cabinet and the overhang should be equal on the sides. Since this cabinet is small, it might be best to clamp the blank in location on the cabinet, then turn the cabinet on its back so you can access the fastener locations more easily (photo 2).

Install the cabinet in the project location. Baseboard and any other obstructions should be removed from the project area. Slip shims below and behind the cabinet as needed to make sure it is level and plumb. Attach the cabinet to the wall by driving 2" wallboard screws through the cabinet back at wall stud locations (photo 3).

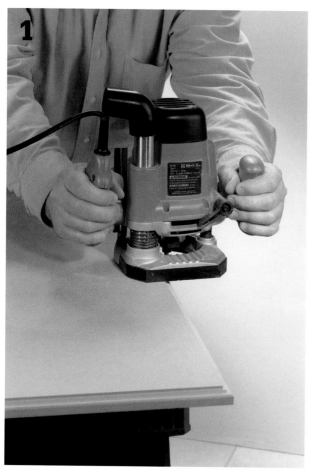

Rout a profile, such as an ogee or roundover, into the sides and front of the seatboard. Use a router table if you have one, otherwise hand-machine it with a piloted profiling bit.

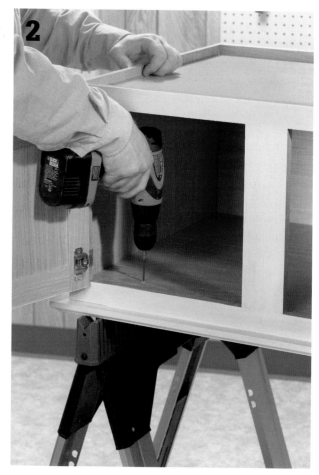

Because these cabinets are so small, it's easier to pre-gang them together, then flip the assembly upside down to install the seatboard.

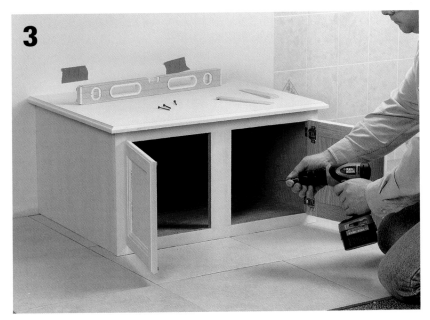

3

Drive screws through the back of the cabinet at the marked wall stud locations.

INSTALL THE PANELING

The backer board for the towel tower can be made from a number of building materials, while retaining the beadboard appearance that lends a bit of country style to this project. The easiest and cheapest product you can use is beadboard paneling: thin sheet stock that comes in 4 × 8 ft. panels. You'll find a wide range of colors, patterns and qualities in the beadboard sheet stock, including some that is pre-sized to around 42" for installation as wainscoting. The cheapest material has a printed pattern layer laminated over hardboard. The better quality material has hardwood veneer over a plywood or lauan backing. We chose real tongue-and-groove boards made from pine. With actual dimensions of ⅜ × 5½", the carsiding product we used has enough depth to create a convincing profile but is still relatively inexpensive.

Because it is very unlikely that the strips of carsiding will be exactly the same width as your base cabinet once they're installed, you'll need to rip-cut the outside boards to fit the project area (it is better to rip-cut both outer boards an equal amount than to take everything out of one of the boards). To gauge where to make your cuts, assemble enough boards to cover the width of the cabinet and lay them out on a flat surface (photo 4). Mark the centerpoint of the middle board and measure out half the distance in each direction. Make rip-cut lines at these points.

Midpoint

Lay out the tongue-and-groove carsiding boards in a row, with the tongues fitted into grooves. Measure out in one direction (half the width of base cabinets) from a midpoint line in the center board.

Project Details

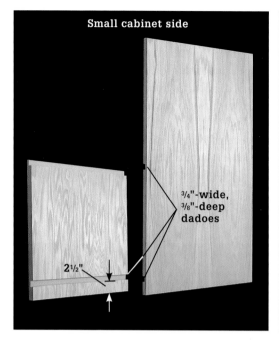

Small cabinet side

¾"-wide, ⅜"-deep dadoes

2½"

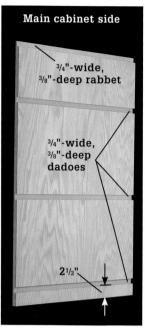

Main cabinet side

¾"-wide, ⅜"-deep rabbet

¾"-wide, ⅜"-deep dadoes

2½"

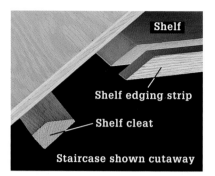

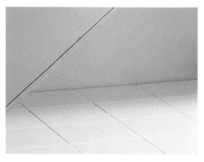

Shelf

Shelf edging strip

Shelf cleat

Staircase shown cutaway

The side panels for the short cabinet (left), made from ¾" plywood, differ in size. A line connecting the tops of the two panels should follow the slope line of the staircase. The side panels for the main cabinets (right), are also made from ¾" plywood, and have dadoes for the cabinet shelves and base, and rabbets for the cabinet top. The taller side panel for the small cabinet fits against a main cabinet side panel when the work center is installed.

Shelves and cleats, made from plywood and 1 × 2 strips, are beveled so they fit flush against the understairs cover. The shelf edging strips are cut from oak 1 × 2, and mitered at the same angle as the shelves.

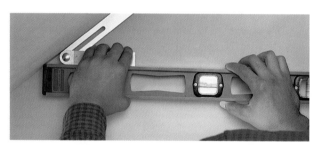

Duplicate the slope of your stairs using a T-bevel. Set one arm of the T-bevel in a level position against the back wall, then align the other arm with the stairs (top photo). Transfer the angle directly to your saw to make mitered and beveled cuts (bottom photo).

Cover stair underside before you install your understairs work center. Panels of 1¾" plywood attached to the stringers of the staircase create an understairs cover that can be used to anchor shelf cleats. If you plan to add electrical or plumbing lines, do the work (or hire a professional if you are inexperienced) before installing your built-in.

How to Build an Understairs Work Center

1

Mark the location for the shelf cleats on the walls and understairs cover, using a level as a guide. Butt the 12" cleats against the back wall, and allow at least 12" of clearance between the countertop and the bottom shelf.

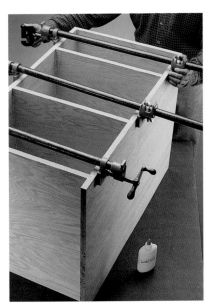

2

Measure and cut 1 × 2 shelf cleats to fit along the reference lines on the walls and the understairs cover (see Project Details, page opposite). Bevel the cleats on the understairs cover to match the stair slope angle. Attach the cleats with 2½" screws.

3

Measure and cut ¾" plywood shelves, then attach a ¾" hardwood strip to each shelf edge (see page opposite) using glue and finish nails. Set shelves on cleats and attach with 1½" finish nails driven through pilot holes.

4

Measure and cut ¾" plywood side panels for main cabinets, then use a router and an edge guide to cut rabbets for top panels and dadoes for bottom panels and shelves (see Project Details, page opposite).

Clamp and glue the cabinet sides to the top and bottom panels and shelves to form rabbet and dado joints. *Note: If you plan to install center-mounted drawer slides, mount slide tracks before you assemble the cabinet.*

6

Reinforce each cabinet joint with 2" finish nails driven at 4" intervals.

Cut a ¼" plywood back panel for each main cabinet. Set each back onto a cabinet frame so that all sides align, then attach them to cabinet side, base, and top panels using 1" wire nails.

Position one cabinet so the top panel is pressed against the understairs cover and front face is flush with edge of stairway. Shim if needed, then toenail into the floor through the side panels, using 2" finish nails. For masonry floors, attach with construction adhesive.

Position the other cabinet ¾" away from side wall, with front face aligned with first cabinet. Check with a level and shim if needed. Insert ¾" spacers between cabinet and side wall, then anchor to wall with 2" screws driven into framing members.

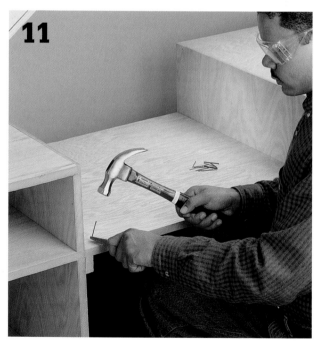

Cut 1 × 2 cleats for the connecting shelf that fits between the main cabinets. Mark level lines on the inner cabinet sides, then attach shelf cleats to the cabinet sides by driving 1¼" screws through counterbored pilot holes.

Measure and cut a ¾" plywood connecting shelf to fit between the cabinets, and attach it to the cleats with 1¼" finish nails. (If you plan to build a drawer using a center-mounted drawer slide, attach the slide track to the shelf before you attach the shelf to the cleats.)

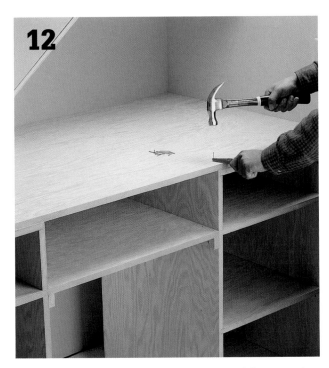

12

Measure and cut a plywood countertop panel that extends all the way to the back wall, with one side flush against the understairs cover. Attach the countertop to top panels of cabinets by driving finish nails down through the countertop.

13

Apply or install any special countertop finishing material, like ceramic tile or plastic laminate. Obtain installation instructions and follow them carefully if you have not installed tile or laminate before.

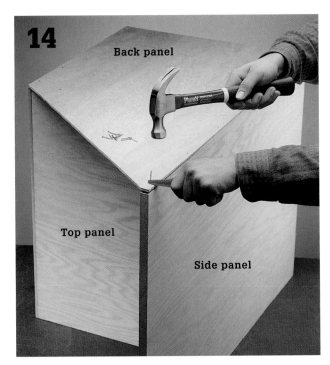

14

Back panel

Top panel

Side panel

Build a small cabinet the same width and depth as the main cabinets (steps 4 to 7). Adjust the height of the side panels to follow the stair slope (see Project Details, page 144). Cut a ¼" plywood back panel, with the top edge sloped at the same angle as the line between the side panel tops. Attach the back panel to the cabinet with 1" wire nails.

15

Position the small cabinet so the taller side panel is flush against the main cabinet. Align the face of the small cabinet with the face of the main cabinet, then check with a level, shimming if necessary. Connect the cabinets by drilling pilot holes, and driving 1¼" screws through the side panels.

If the corner is open at the bottom of the stairs, attach nailing strips to the understairs cover and cabinet sides, then cut a plywood panel to fit the space, and attach it to the nailing strips with 1" screws.

Measure and cut 1 × 3 bottom rails for the cabinets. Also cut a long, diagonal rail to fit along the edge of the understairs cover. Miter the ends of the diagonal rail to fit against the floor and the side wall, and miter the longer bottom rail to form a clean joint with the diagonal rail. Test-fit the rails, then attach them with glue and 2" finish nails driven through pilot holes.

Measure and cut 1 × 3 rails to cover the edges of the connecting shelf and the countertop. Miter the end of the countertop rail that joins the long, diagonal rail. Attach the shelf and countertop rails flush with the countertop and shelf surfaces, using glue and 2" finish nails driven through pilot holes.

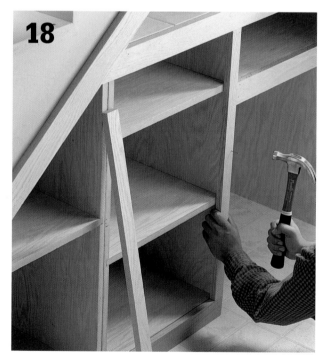

Measure and cut 1 × 2 stiles for the front edges of the cabinets. Attach the stiles, flush with the edges of the cabinet sides, using glue and 2" finish nails driven through pilot holes.

Measure and cut 1 × 2 rails to fit between the stiles, so they cover the cabinet shelf edges and are flush with the shelf tops. Attach the rails, using glue and 2" finish nails driven through pilot holes.

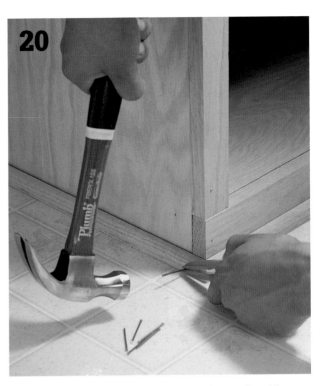

Cut base-shoe molding to cover gaps along wall and floor surfaces, mitering the corners. Tack the molding, using 2" finish nails. Sand, fill, and finish the understairs center.

Attach slide tracks for side-mounted drawer slides, according to the manufacturer's directions.

Build, finish, and install drawers (see pages 48 to 49) and drawer hardware. Purchase or build and finish cabinet doors and hang them using ⅜" semi-concealed hinges.

Attach drawer slide tracks to the center of the bottom panel and the shelves, following manufacturer's directions.

Clamp and glue the shelves to the side panels to form butt joints. Reinforce the joints with 2" screws driven through the side panels and into the edges of shelves.

Clamp and glue the top and bottom panels to the side panels, then reinforce the joints with 2" screws.

Measure and cut ¼" plywood panel to cover the back of the cabinet. Attach with 1" screws or wire nails driven through the back and into the side, top, and bottom panels.

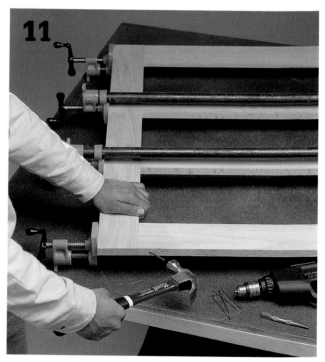

Measure the width and height between the inside edges of the cabinet. Cut the rails to the width. Cut the stiles to the height plus 7". Clamp and glue rails between stiles, and reinforce joints by toenailing 3" finish nails through the rails and into the stiles.

12

Apply glue to the edges of the cabinet, then position the face frame over the cabinet so the inside edges of the face frame are flush with the top, bottom, and side panels. Attach the face frame by drilling pilot holes and driving 1½" finish nails into the cabinet every 8". Use a nail set to countersink the nail heads.

13

Slide the cabinet into the opening so it rests on the pedestals and the face frame is against the wall surface.

14

Anchor the cabinet by drilling pilot holes and driving 3" finish nails through the face frame and into the wall framing members. Also, drive 3" finish nails through the bottom of the cabinet and into the sill.

15

Sand and finish the cabinet face frame, then build, finish, and install overlay drawers (pages 48 to 49).

SHELVING
PROJECTS

Shelving Basics

When making shelves for your floor-to-ceiling shelves or utility shelves, choose shelving materials appropriate for the loads they must support. Thin glass shelves or particleboard can easily support light loads, such as decorative glassware, but only the sturdiest shelves can hold a large television set or heavy reference books without bending or breaking.

The strength of a shelf depends on its span—the distance between vertical risers. In general, the span should be no more than 36" long.

Building your own shelves from finish-grade plywood edged with hardwood strips is a good choice for most carpentry projects. Edged plywood shelves are strong, attractive, and much less expensive than solid hardwood shelves.

Tools & Materials ▸

Right-angle drill guide
Drill with bits
Marking gauge
Router
Hammer
Nail set
Shelving material

Scrap pegboard
Pin-style shelf
 supports
Metal shelf
 standards
Shelf clips
Finish nails

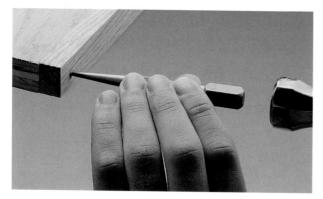

Attach hardwood edging or moldings to the front face of plywood shelves, using wood glue and finish nails. Position the edging so the top is slightly above the plywood surface, then drill pilot holes and drive finish nails. Use a nail set to countersink the nail heads. Sand the edging so it is smooth with the plywood surface before you finish the shelf. For greater strength, edge plywood shelves with 1 × 2 or 1 × 3 hardwood boards.

¼" glass

Melamine-covered particleboard

¾" pine

¾" finish-grade plywood

¾" hardwood

¾" finish-grade plywood edged with 1 × 2 hardwood

Double-layer plywood edged with hardwood molding

Shelves shown in order of strength

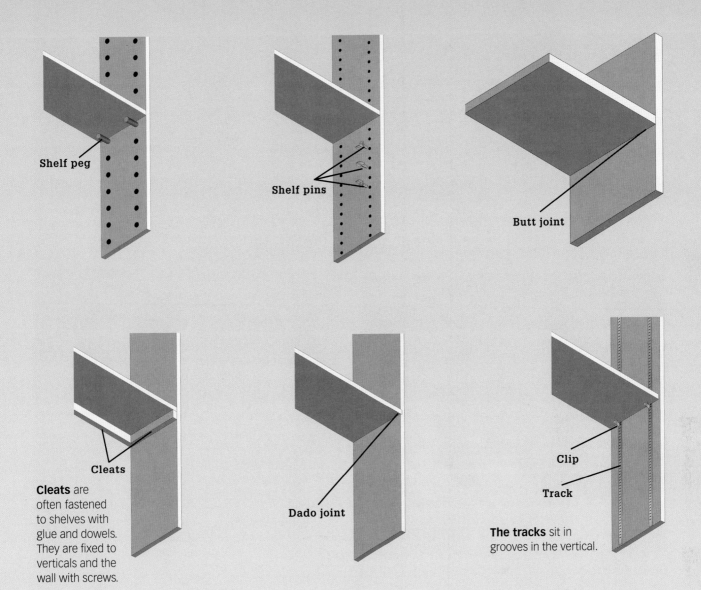

Shelf peg

Shelf pins

Butt joint

Cleats are often fastened to shelves with glue and dowels. They are fixed to verticals and the wall with screws.

Cleats

Dado joint

Clip

Track

The tracks sit in grooves in the vertical.

L-bracket

There are several types of L-brackets available at home centers. Choose the bracket most suitable for the weight load of shelving.

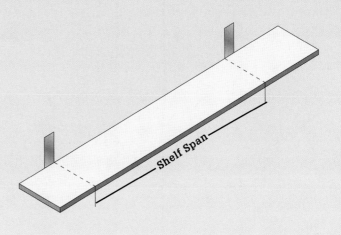

Shelf Span

Shelf span is the distance between risers. A shorter span strengthens a shelf.

Modular Shelving

Shelving is not a one-size-fits-all proposition. Your beer can collection has entirely different shelving needs from your Encyclopedia Brittanica volumes, which in turn have equally different demands from your paperback novels. The beauty of making your own shelving is that you can easily customize both the size and the support mechanism to your needs.

One good way to customize shelving is to make modular shelves with adjustable supports.

While display shelves can be as narrow as a couple of inches, typical storage shelves range between 11" (bookcases) and 24" (closet or cabinet depth). In this section you'll learn how to make and finish custom shelves to any width you choose.

Great for closets and utility storage, modular shelves are supported by adjustable pins or brackets so you can easily increase or decrease the space between shelves to meet your storage needs.

Tips for Making Shelves ▶

Rip-cut shelves to the exact width you need from sheet stock. Quality plywood offers the most strength, but for ease of cleaning you'll appreciate melamine-coated particleboard.

Heat-activated veneer edge tape can be applied to the edges of plywood or particleboard shelves for a more finished appearance.

How to Install Pin-style Supports for Adjustable Shelves

Mount a drill and ¼" bit in a right-angle drill guide, with the drill-stop set for ⅜" cutting depth. Align a pegboard scrap along the inside face of each shelf standard, exactly flush with the end, to use as a template. Drill two rows of parallel holes in each riser, about 1½" from the edges of riser, using the pegboard holes as a guide.

When the bookcase or built-in is completed, build shelves that are ¼" shorter than the distance between standards. To mount each shelf, insert a pair of ¼" pin-style shelf supports in each riser.

How to Install Metal Standards for Adjustable Shelves

Mark two parallel dado grooves on the inside face of each standard, using a marking gauge. Grooves should be at least 1" from the edges.

Cut dadoes to depth and thickness of metal tracks, using a router. Test-fit tracks to make sure they fit, then remove them.

After finishing the built-in, cut metal tracks to length to fit into dadoes and attach them using nails or screws provided by the manufacturer. Make sure slots in tracks are aligned properly so shelves will be level.

Make shelves so they are ⅛" shorter than the distance between standards, then insert shelf clips into the slots in the metal tracks, and install shelves.

How to Build Utility Shelves

1

Mark the location of top plates on ceiling. One plate should be flush against wall, and the other should be parallel to first plate, with the front edge 24" from the wall. Cut 2 × 4 top plates to full length of utility shelves, then attach to ceiling joists or blocking, using 3" screws.

2

Mark points directly beneath outside corners of the top plates to find outer sole plate locations, using a plumb bob as a guide (top). Mark sole plate locations by drawing lines perpendicular to the wall connecting each pair of points (bottom).

3

Cut outer 2 × 4 sole plates and position them perpendicular to the wall, just inside the outlines. Shim plates to level if needed, then attach to floor with a powder-actuated nailer or 3" screws. Attach a center sole plate midway between the outer sole plates.

4

Prepare the shelf risers by cutting ⅞"-wide, ¾"-deep dadoes with a router. Cut dadoes every 4" along the inside face of each 2 × 4 riser, with the top and bottom dadoes cut about 12" from the ends of the 2 × 4. Tip: Gang-cut the risers by laying them flat and clamping them together, then attaching an edge guide (page 41) to align the dado cuts. For each cut, make several passes with the router, gradually extending the bit depth until dadoes are ¾" deep.

5

Trim the shelf risers to uniform length before unclamping them. Use a circular saw and a straightedge guide.

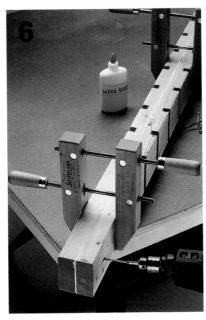

Build two center shelf supports by positioning pairs of shelf risers back-to-back and joining them with wood glue and 2½" screws.

Build four end shelf supports by positioning the back of a dadoed shelf riser against a 2 × 4 of the same length, then joining the 2 × 4 and the riser with glue and 2½" screws.

Position an end shelf support at each corner of the shelving unit, between top and sole plates. Attach the supports by driving 3" screws toenail-style into the top plate and sole plates.

Position a center shelf support (both faces dadoed) at each end of the center sole plate, then anchor shelf supports to the sole plate using 3" screws driven toenail-style. Use a framing square to align the center shelf supports perpendicular to the top plates, then anchor to top plates.

Measure the distance between the facing dado grooves and subtract ¼". Cut the plywood shelves to fit and slide the shelves into the grooves.

ASSEMBLE THE SHELF

Set two of the bevel-cut workpieces up in the assembly jig. Dry-fit the corner to see that it fits and the joint is tight. If it's not, something is off and an adjustment is required.

Apply glue to both ends and re-create the joint. Reinforce with finish nails driven with a pneumatic brad nailer (photo 4). Fasten the other two workpieces in the same fashion, and then attach the two L-shapes to form the finished square (photo 5). Make sure you wipe away all glue squeeze-out with a damp cloth or sponge and allow it to dry.

INSTALL HANGING HARDWARE

The cube-shape boxes look most impressive if they are mounted on the wall with no visible means of support. A good method for accomplishing this is to hang them

with keyhole-style picture frame hangers that fit into recessed cuts in the back edges of the box. To hang the box with this hardware, position the box on the worksurface with the back edges up. Then, drill a ¼"-deep by ⁵⁄₁₆"-dia. hole that's 3" from each end along the edge you want to be on top. Chisel out a ⅛"-deep, ½"-wide × ¾"-long mortise that's centered over each hole and stops just shy of the edges of the board (photo 6).

Place the hanger in the slot over the pre-drilled hole and mark the screw holes with a pencil. Pre-drill the hanger holes and install the hangers, using a screwdriver to prevent overdriving (photo 7).

FINISH & HANG THE SHELF

Apply your finish of choice and allow it to dry. Treating all faces of the shelf will help prevent environmental forces (like humidity and temperature change) from

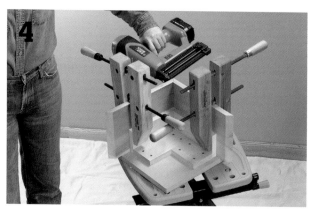

After testing the fit, glue the first miter joint together and reinforce it with an air nailer (if you must hand-nail, carefully drill pilots holes first). Use the assembly jig to square up the workpieces.

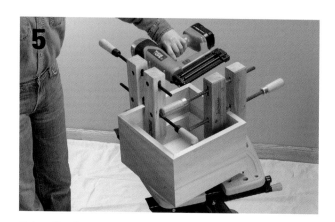

Using the jig, assemble both L's with glue and fasteners.

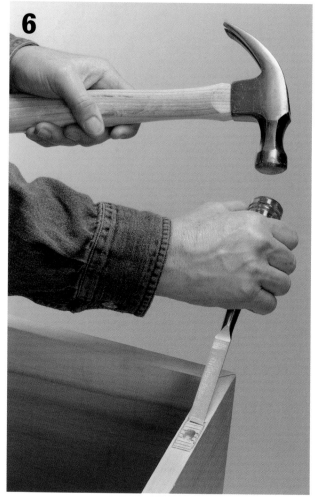

Cut a mortise for the body of the hanger hardware to rest in. Be sure not to cut through to the edge of the shelf so the connection will be invisible once the box is mounted.

opening the joints. Set the cube shelf level on the wall and mark the locations for the screws that will fit into the keyhole picture hangers. Drill guide holes for plastic wall anchors at the hanger locations and drive round-head wood screws so they leave a gap of about ⅛" between the screw head and the wall. Slip the box over the screwheads and tug downward to secure it (photo 8).

Stepback box variation ▸

Making cube-shaped shelves can take you further than single layer display shelves, enabling you to add layers and depth to your display boxes and the items in them. In other words, some photos look great in a plain frame while others call out for more detail. The good news is that adding detail to the shelf doesn't require a major re-tooling of your set-up. You can still use all kinds of materials, including MDF (shown here), though sizing down to smaller stock for smaller shelves looks more proportional. And, because this version is layered, you can mix and match species to create an eye-catching color contrast.

Since there are 16 pieces in this system (not four) as in the project box—the easiest and fastest way to make accurate cuts is to cut and shape the stock for both the inner cube and outer cube, and then laminate them together with glue so the front edges are oriented correctly and the back edges are flush. Then, simply cut the workpieces, bevel the ends and assemble the cube as shown in the main sequence.

This 16-piece variation of the cube shelf has the added feature of shadow lines created by the stepped back sides.

Pre-drill the hanger holes and install the hanger hardware using a screwdriver or a drill/driver and a light touch.

Drive roundhead screws into the wall, using sleeves or anchors as needed. Then hang the keyhole hanger hardware mounted to the back of the shelf onto the screwheads.

Closet Shelves

This simple project will more than double the storage potential in a small linen or pantry closet. It is perfect for light loads in closets with a span of 36" or less. The 1 × 3 furring strips are inexpensive and easy to install, and the shelving seen from the outside of the door lends a professional touch. If you don't have a lot of time, but would like to try your hand at an installation to maximize your storage, start here.

Tools & Materials ▸

Stud finder
Tape measure
Level
Screwdriver
Jig saw
Nail gun
6d and 8d finish nails

¾"-thick shelving
  stock (without
  predrilled holes)
1 × 3 pine
Wood screws
L-brackets (optional)
Finish materials

How to Install Closet Shelves

Measure from the floor up 15" and mark a level line. Repeat level lines every 12" up from original line (repeat four times for an 80"-tall closet) (photo 1).

Cut 1 × 3 strips to fit along the back side of the wall, flush into each corner. Cut 1 × 3 strips to fit along walls, flush against the back wall 1 × 3 strips and 4" short of the inside wall (approximately 6" in from closet door track). Align the tops of 1 × 3 strips with level lines on wall and fasten to the wall, hitting studs where possible (photo 2). *Note: If you cannot hit a stud, use a self-driving metal anchor with machine screws every 10".*

Cut melamine shelving stock (without pre-drilled holes) to fit along the back side wall (measure wall and subtract 4"). Rest shelves on top of the 1 × 3 strips (photo 3).

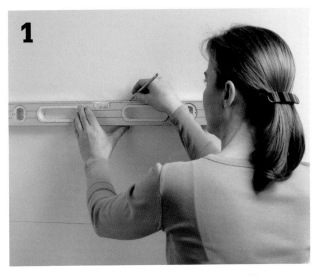

Measure from the floor up 15" and mark a level line. Repeat level lines every 12" up from original line (repeat four times for an 80"-tall closet).

Fasten 1 × 3 strips to back side wall, flush into each corner, and fasten 1 × 3 strips along the side wall (as shown, ending approximately 6" in from door track). Align the tops of the 1 × 3 strips with level lines on wall and fasten to wall with a nail gun at studs. *Note:* If you cannot hit a stud, use a self-driving metal anchor with machine screw every 10".

Cut melamine-coated shelving stock (without predrilled holes) to fit along back side wall (measure wall and subtract 4"). Rest shelves on top of 1 × 3 strips.

How to Make Joist Shelving

Before you begin cutting the pieces for the frame of the joist shelving, measure the space between the joists where you plan to install the unit. Standard construction should leave a 14½" space between ceiling joists. However, depending on how old the wood is and how your house has settled, the space between your joists could be anywhere from 12" to 16". Make sure you know those dimensions so you can plan the rest of the box construction accordingly.

MAKE THE BOX

Measure and cut the sides (A), top (B), bottom (C), and middle shelf (D) of the box frame to size from 1 × 6 pine lumber and sand the edges smooth. Position the sides, top, and bottom panels with their back edges on the work surface, with the perimeter of the box flush at the outer edges.

Drill counterbored pilot holes through the bottom and top panels into the side panels and assemble the frame, using glue and wood screws driven through the ends and into the sides (photo 1).

Using a combination square as a guide, mark a reference line across the interior face of each side panel, 15¼" up from the top of the bottom panel. These lines represent the bottom of the shelf.

Slide the middle shelf into position so the bottom edge is flush with the reference lines. Drill counterbored pilot holes through the sides and into the shelf. Attach the shelf using glue and screws.

Cut the shelf rails (F) to the proper length and sand the edges smooth. Mark reference lines for the shelf rails 6" up from the top of the bottom panel and 6" up from the top of the middle shelf.

Assemble the frame of the box, using glue and 1½" wood screws.

Clamp the shelf in place between the joists and drill holes for the carriage bolts.

Insert a carriage bolt through the shelf walls and joists, then add a washer, lock washer, and hex nut.

Attach the rails so their top edges are flush with the reference lines and the front surface of the rail is flush with the sides. Drill counterbored pilot holes through the rails and into the sides and attach them, using glue and wood screws. Cut the back panel (E) to size and attach it to the back edges of the box frame, using glue and wood screws.

DRILL HOLES THROUGH THE JOISTS

Refer to the top inset of the diagram on page 207 for specific instructions on the location of the swinging assembly holes.

Clamp the unit into position between the joists so it is level and so the top of the shelf is approximately 3" from the subfloor above. When the shelf is in position and clamped tightly, drill a ½" hole on either side of the shelf, through the joists and into the shelf (photo 2).

INSTALL THE SWINGING ASSEMBLY

Slide the carriage bolts through the holes from the interior of the shelf, and thread a flat washer, lock washer, and nut onto the carriage bolt until they are snug, using a ratchet set if necessary (photo 3). Do not overtighten the assembly or the shelf will not rotate.

Test the shelf by rotating it up into the ceiling, making sure it glides easily between the joists. With a pencil, make a reference mark on both joists, approximately 2" in from the bottom edge of the shelf in the up position.

INSTALL THE CLEATS

Cut the scrap piece of ¾" plywood into two pieces approximately ¾ × 1½ × 4". Use two ¼ × 2" lag screws to attach the scrap pieces of plywood to the bottom edges of the joists so that the edges are flush with the inside edges of the joists (photo 4). The scrap pieces should be tight but still easy to rotate. Rotate cleats to hold the shelf in its closed position.

> ## Variation ▸
>
> If you want a deeper shelf (photo 5), use the same construction method, but alter the dimensions. Install this larger box by driving four lag screws through the joists. The shelf will be stationary, but it will still utilize space near the ceiling. See the bottom inset diagram on page 207.

> ## Warning ▸
>
> The shelf must be clamped tightly in place; otherwise, it may fall during installation. Do not place weight on the shelf until it is completely installed, or you could risk injury.

Screw plywood cleats into position to act as latches for the shelf.

To build a deeper, stationary shelf, build the unit with wider lumber, and drive two ½ × 2" lag bolts through each side of the shelf and into the adjoining joists.

Bin & Shelving Unit

This versatile wall accessory offers clever storage space for rolled hand towels, soaps, and other small items. The unit can be custom-designed to fit the available wall space and depth for any room. In areas with less wall space, a shorter unit may be built by making only two V-sections. Or, add more V-sections for a larger wall space. For even more versatility, the V-sections may be mounted in stair-step fashion.

Store smaller items in the bins of this shelving unit, reducing clutter on your countertop or vanity.

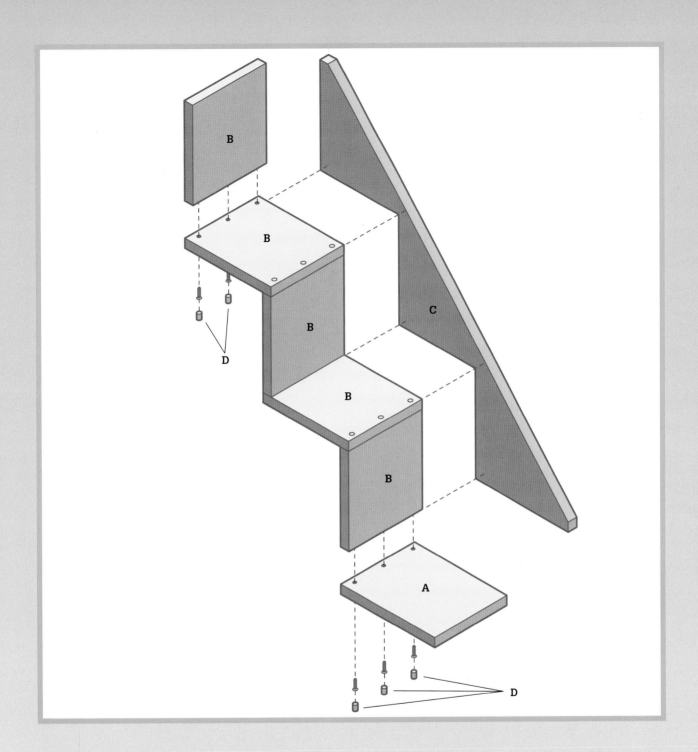

Tools

Miter saw
Jig saw
Clamps
Drill with bits
#8 adjustable counterbore bit
Hammer
Small hand saw
Stud finder

Materials

1 × 6" × 4 ft. pine
1 × 8" × 4 ft. pine
⅜"-dia. dowel
Cotton swabs
Wallboard screws (#8 × 1⅝")
Wood glue
Finishing materials
Sandpaper

Cutting List

Key	Part	Dimension
A	(1) Shelf panel	¾ × 5½ × 8¼" lumber
B	(5) Shelf panel	¾ × 5½ × 7½" lumber
C	(1) Backer board	¾ × 7¼" × 3 ft. lumber
D	(15) Dowel pieces	⅜"-dia × ½" dowel

How to Make a Bin & Shelving Unit

CUT SHELF PANELS & ASSEMBLE A V-SECTION

Cut the longer shelf panel (A) and all five additional shelf panels (B) to size using a miter saw. Sand any rough edges smooth using 150-grit sandpaper.

Position the panels on the table as they will be assembled, checking the fit and layout of each panel. Make sure the longer shelf panel (A) is farthest to the right of the assembly.

Clamp the longer shelf panel (A) to one of the regular shelf panels (B) at a right angle so that the edges are flush against the worksurface (photo 1).

Adjust a #8 counterbore bit to a total depth of 2". Drill three equally spaced counterbored pilot holes through the longer shelf, ⅜" from the lower edge. Each hole should have a ¼" counterbore. Drive 1⅝" wallboard screws into each hole of the clamped assembly.

ATTACH THE REMAINING SHELF PANELS

Attach each remaining shelf panel at a right angle, repeating the construction methods described in the first step. Clamp each new shelf to the workpiece so that the new shelf is flush against the worksurface, with the side edges of each new panel flush with the side edges of the workpiece (photo 2).

PREPARE THE BACKER BOARD

Lay the completed shelf assembly on the backer board, so that the top point of each V-section is flush with the backer board's top edge.

Trace the outline of the V-sections on the backer board and cut along the lower cutting lines using a jig saw (photo 3).

Draw lines on the front of the backer board showing the locations of the wallboard screws in the V-section assembly.

Mark the position for three screws along each side of the V-sections, avoiding the lines made for the wallboard screws inside the V-sections. Then drill holes through the backer board at the placement marks, using ⅛" drill bit.

INSTALL THE BACKER BOARD

Place unit on the table, with the front edge facing down. Turn the backer board over, and position it on top of the workpiece, aligning the edges.

Keeping the unit aligned with the backer board, drill a pilot hole in the placement mark closest to the center of the middle V-section with the adjustable counterbore bit. Only drill deep enough with the bit to create a countersink for the head of the screw.

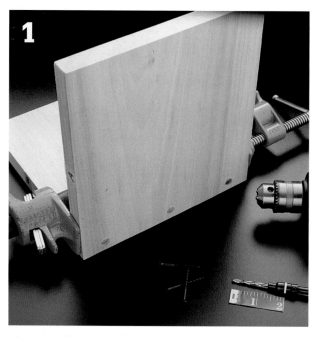

Clamp shelf A to shelf B and drill three equally spaced counterbored pilot holes through shelf A into shelf B.

Clamp each new shelf to the workpiece so that the new shelf is flush against the worksurface.

Drive a wallboard screw into the countersunk pilot hole (photo 4) and recheck the alignment of the two pieces.

Drill and countersink the remaining pilot holes and drive wallboard screws through the holes into the V-sections, starting with the ends of the unit and working your way back toward the center.

APPLY THE FINISHING TOUCHES

Cut a ⅜" dowel into ½" lengths to use as wood plugs for the counterbored holes. Bevel one end of each plug by sanding or filing it slightly.

Place a small amount of wood glue in the counterbored holes using a cotton swab. Insert a wood plug into each hole, beveled end first, and tap it in place with a hammer or a rubber mallet (photo 5). Wipe away any excess glue using a dampened cloth. Allow the glue to dry overnight.

Sand the outer edges of the backer board and edges of the shelves. Cut off the excess of the plugs after the glue has dried using a small hand saw. The plugs should only extend slightly from the surface. Take care not to scratch the wood surface when trimming the plugs.

Sand the plugs flush with the surface, using 80-grit sandpaper on a sanding block. Sand the entire unit until smooth, using fine-grit sandpaper.

Paint the unit or apply the stain of your choice and a clear acrylic finish. Let the finish dry according to the manufacturer's instructions.

To mount the shelving unit, locate studs in the wall to use as mounting points. If no studs are available, make sure to use the proper type of wall fastener.

Variation ▶

Using the same assembly steps, make a diagonal shelving unit as shown on page 210. Increase the "step up" effect by cutting the shelf panels to graduated lengths. Cut the lowest shelf at 8¼" long, the second shelf at 7½" long, the next two at 6½", and the last two at 5½" long. Then hang the shelf on the wall diagonally. The graduated shelves allow you to place heavier, larger objects on the lower shelves and lighter more decorative pieces above.

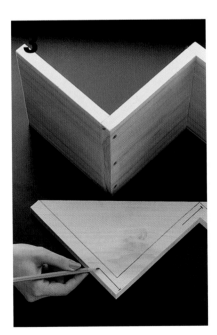

Mark lines on the backer board front indicating where the V-sections are screwed together. Then mark reference lines for three screws along each section.

Position the backer board over the workpiece, aligning the edges, and drive screws through countersunk pilot holes starting with the hole closest to the center.

Tap the wood plugs into the counterbored holes. Allow the glue to dry, and trim the wood plugs using a small hand saw.

Trimwork Wall Shelves

Here's a neat trick: Build a shelf that stores, displays and elevates your favorite collectibles and knick knacks so they're well within sight but safely out of the way. Building these built-up projects is a fun mix of rough and finish carpentry. We show you how to make two variations here: one is a mass of stepped-back MDF strips that has real presence when painted. The other is a more refined three-part assembly similar to cornice molding that is made with pine and pine moldings and boasts a clear wood finish. The feature both shelves share is a broad, flat surface that performs as a handy display shelf.

If you're building the crown molding version of this project, one skill you may wish to brush up on ahead of time is cutting and coping crown molding. Working with crown molding requires some mental gymnastics, but once you learn the floor routine you'll be glad you did.

You can hang your new shelves at just about any height, although they naturally look more comfortable higher up on the wall. At least try and position them at or slightly above eye level. Locating the shelves so the bottom edge rests on top of a door head casing is one good strategy.

In this project we detail two basic interpretations of the shelving strategy. Both are essentially built-up box beams, although one uses crown molding as the featured trim while the other is based on stepped-back strips of stock. There are also different variations on how the shelf can be installed. For example, you can wrap the entire room with it, simply span from one wall to another, or place it on three walls only, etc. Not only is this built-in totally home-made, but the design is flexible to suit different needs and tastes.

And by choosing trim types and styles that already are present in your home you can enhance the built-in look.

The two styles of trimwork shelves seen here are constructed with simple butt joints for ease of building. If you have the woodworking equipment and skills, consider using dado joints instead of butt joints where it makes sense. With dado joints, the wood parts can expand and contract (as they are prone to) without creating separation gaps.

How to Build Floor-to-Ceiling Shelves

Mark the location for two parallel 2 × 4 top plates on the ceiling, using a framing square as a guide. The front edge of the outer top plate should be 13" from the back wall, and the other top plate should be flush against the wall. Mark the location of the ceiling joists; if necessary, install blocking between joists to provide a surface for anchoring the top plates.

Measure and cut the 2 × 4 top plates. Position each plate, check to make sure it is level, and install shims if necessary. Attach the plates to the ceiling with 3" screws driven into the joists or blocking.

Cut 2 × 4 sole plates and screw them together to form two doubled sole plates. Use a plumb bob suspended from the outside corners of the top plates to align the sole plates. Shim the plates to level, if needed. Anchor the plates by driving 3" screws toenail-style into the floor.

Install 2 × 4 support studs between the ends of the top plates and sole plates. Attach support studs with 3" screws driven toenail-style into the top plates and sole plates.

Install the center support studs midway between the end support studs. Attach them to the bottom plate first, using 3" screws driven toenail-style. Use a level to make sure that each stud is plumb, then attach the studs to the top plate with 3" screws.

Where the shelves fit into a corner, use 1⅝" screws to attach ½" plywood spacers on the inside faces of the support studs, spaced every 4". Make sure spacers do not extend past the front face of the studs.

Where the end of the project is exposed, measure and cut a ½" plywood end panel to floor-to-ceiling height. Attach the panel to the support studs so the front edges are flush, using 1¾" screws driven through the support studs and into the end panel.

Measure and cut ½" plywood top and bottom panels to fit between the support studs. Attach to the top and sole plates using 1½" finish nails.

Measure and cut lower risers from ½" plywood, then cut dadoes for metal shelf standards using an edge guide (page 41).

Install lower risers on each side of the 2 × 4 support studs so the front edges are flush with the edges of the studs. Attach risers with 1½" finish nails driven into the support studs. For risers that adjoin the wall, drive nails at spacer locations.

Measure and cut permanent shelves from ¾" plywood to fit between the support studs, just above the lower risers. Set the shelves on the risers and attach them with 1½" finish nails driven down into the risers.

Measure and cut upper risers to fit between the permanent shelves and the top panels. Cut dadoes for metal shelf standards, then attach the risers to the support studs with 1½" finish nails.

Measure and cut 1 × 3 stiles to reach from floor to ceiling along the front edges of the exposed support studs. Drill pilot holes and attach the stiles to the support studs so they are flush with the risers, using glue and 1½" finish nails driven at 8" intervals.

Measure and cut 1 × 3 top rails to fit between the stiles. Drill pilot holes and attach the rails to the top plate and top panels, using carpenter's glue and 1½" finish nails.

Measure and cut 1 × 4 bottom rails to fit between the stiles. Drill pilot holes, and attach the rails to the sole plates and bottom panels, using glue and 1½" finish nails. The top edge of the rails should be flush with the top surface of the plywood panels.

Fill nail holes, then sand and finish the wood surfaces.

Measure, cut, and install metal shelf standards into the dadoes, using nails or screws provided by the manufacturer.

Measure and cut adjustable shelves ⅛" shorter than the distance between metal standards. Cut shelf edging, and attach it with glue and 1½" finish nails. Sand and finish the shelves.

Insert shelf clips into the metal shelf standards and install the adjustable shelves at desired heights.

Cover gaps between the project and walls and floor with molding that has been finished to match the shelf unit.

Photo Credits

Aristokraft Cabinetry
© Aristokraft Cabinetry; p. 6
www.aristokraft.com

Todd Caverly
© Todd Caverly for Judy Ostrow, Designer; p. 7 (right)
© Todd Caverly for G. M. Wild Construction, Inc.; pp.10, 15 (bottom left)
© Todd Caverly; p. 15 (top)

Diamond Cabinets
© Diamond Cabinets, a division of MasterBrand Cabinets, Inc.; pp. 5, 9
www.diamondcabinets.com

Focal Point Architectural Products
© Focal Point Architectural Products; p. 7 (left)
www.focalpointap.com

KraftMaid Cabinetry, Inc.
© KraftMaid Cabinetry, Inc.; pp.13, 16 (bottom)
www.kraftmaid.com

Omega Cabinetry
© Omega Cabinetry; p. 15 (bottom right)
www.omegacab.com

Quality Cabinets
© Quality Cabinets; p. 14
www.qualitycabinets.com

Quentin Harriot
© Quentin Harriot/www.ewastock.com; p. 17

Brian VandenBrink
© Brian VandenBrink for Elliott Elliott Norelius Architects; p. 8 (top)
© Brian VandenBrink for Brett Donham Architect; p. 8 (bottom)
© Brian VandenBrink for Centerbrook Architects; p. 12 (top)
© Brian VandenBrink for Lo Yi Chan Architect; p. 12 (bottom)

Wellborn Cabinet, Inc.
© Wellborn Cabinet, Inc., pp.11 (both), 16 (top)
www.wellborn.com

Index

Conversion Charts

Converting Measurements

To Convert:	To:	Multiply by:
Inches	Millimeters	25.4
Inches	Centimeters	2.54
Feet	Meters	0.305
Yards	Meters	0.914
Square inches	Square centimeters	6.45
Square feet	Square meters	0.093
Square yards	Square meters	0.836
Cubic inches	Cubic centimeters	16.4
Cubic feet	Cubic meters	0.0283
Cubic yards	Cubic meters	0.765
Ounces	Milliliters	30.0
Pints (U.S.)	Liters	0.473 (Imp. 0.568)
Quarts (U.S.)	Liters	0.946 (Imp. 1.136)
Gallons (U.S.)	Liters	3.785 (Imp. 4.546)
Ounces	Grams	28.4
Pounds	Kilograms	0.454

To Convert:	To:	Multiply by:
Millimeters	Inches	0.039
Centimeters	Inches	0.394
Meters	Feet	3.28
Meters	Yards	1.09
Square centimeters	Square inches	0.155
Square meters	Square feet	10.8
Square meters	Square yards	1.2
Cubic centimeters	Cubic inches	0.061
Cubic meters	Cubic feet	35.3
Cubic meters	Cubic yards	1.31
Milliliters	Ounces	.033
Liters	Pints (U.S.)	2.114 (Imp. 1.76)
Liters	Quarts (U.S.)	1.057 (Imp. 0.88)
Liters	Gallons (U.S.)	0.264 (Imp. 0.22)
Grams	Ounces	0.035
Kilograms	Pounds	2.2

Lumber Dimensions

Nominal - U.S.	Actual - U.S.	METRIC
1 × 2	¾ × 1½"	19 × 38 mm
1 × 3	¾ × 2½"	19 × 64 mm
1 × 4	¾ × 3½"	19 × 89 mm
1 × 5	¾ × 4½"	19 × 114 mm
1 × 6	¾ × 5½"	19 × 140 mm
1 × 7	¾ × 6¼"	19 × 159 mm
1 × 8	¾ × 7¼"	19 × 184 mm
1 × 10	¾ × 9¼"	19 × 235 mm
1 × 12	¾ × 11¼"	19 × 286 mm
1¼ × 4	1 × 3½"	25 × 89 mm
1¼ × 6	1 × 5½"	25 × 140 mm
1¼ × 8	1 × 7¼"	25 × 184 mm
1¼ × 10	1 × 9¼"	25 × 235 mm
1¼ × 12	1 × 11¼"	25 × 286 mm
1½ × 4	1¼ × 3½"	32 × 89 mm
1½ × 6	1¼ × 5½"	32 × 140 mm
1½ × 8	1¼ × 7¼"	32 × 184 mm
1½ × 10	1¼ × 9¼"	32 × 235 mm
1½ × 12	1¼ × 11¼"	32 × 286 mm
2 × 4	1½ × 3½"	38 × 89 mm
2 × 6	1½ × 5½"	38 × 140 mm
2 × 8	1½ × 7¼"	38 × 184 mm
2 × 10	1½ × 9¼"	38 × 235 mm
2 × 12	1½ × 11¼"	38 × 286 mm
3 × 6	2½ × 5½"	64 × 140 mm
4 × 4	3½ × 3½"	89 × 89 mm
4 × 6	3½ × 5½"	89 × 140 mm

Liquid Measurement Equivalents

1 Pint	= 16 Fluid Ounces	= 2 Cups
1 Quart	= 32 Fluid Ounces	= 2 Pints
1 Gallon	= 128 Fluid Ounces	= 4 Quarts

Converting Temperatures

Convert degrees Fahrenheit (F) to degrees Celsius (C) by following this simple formula: Subtract 32 from the Fahrenheit temperature reading. Then, multiply that number by ⁵⁄₉. For example, 77°F - 32 = 45. 45 × ⁵⁄₉ = 25°C.

To convert degrees Celsius to degrees Fahrenheit, multiply the Celsius temperature reading by ⁹⁄₅. Then, add 32. For example, 25°C × ⁹⁄₅ = 45. 45 + 32 = 77°F.

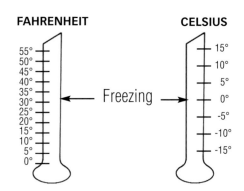

FAHRENHEIT — Freezing → CELSIUS